Cooking With the Micheff Sisters

A Vegan Vegetarian Cookbook

Edited by Aileen Andrès Sox

Designed by Michelle C. Petz

Cover photos: *Front* (food) © Getty Images; (sisters' portrait) Tammy Larsen

Back (background food) Mark Mosrie; (snapshot) Tammy Larsen

Interior food photos by Mark Mosrie

Food styling for interior photos and back cover background by Whitney Kemp

Additional copies of this book are available by calling toll free 1.800.765.6955
or visiting www.AdventistBookCenter.com

ISBN: 0-8163-1994-4

04 05 06 07 08 • 5 4 3 2 1

Cooking With the Micheff Sisters

A Vegan Vegetarian Cookbook

Pacific Press® Publishing Association
Nampa, Idaho
Oshawa, Ontario, Canada

www.PacificPress.com

Foreword

Julia Outkina and the Micheff sisters visited Julia's brother, Boris Nemtsov, at the Duma in Moscow. Boris was the Vice President of Parliament at the time this photo was taken.

If you are interested in healthy cooking and happy living, you've got the right book. I say this because I have observed the experiences of hundreds of people who have attended the Micheff sisters' cooking seminars. I also say it as one viewer among probable millions of viewers around the world who watch their cooking shows on 3ABN.

When the Micheff sisters came to Russia, it changed our lives. They showed us how to have a healthier lifestyle and also how to laugh and have fun. Russian women work hard not only in the home but outside the home as well. After working all day, it is difficult for them to come home and fix meals for their families. But this all changed for the hundreds of women, men, and children who came to the Micheff sisters' cooking school here in Nizhni, Novgorod.

For the first time I saw the women enjoy cooking! They helped the Micheff sisters make recipes, and everyone was laughing and having so much fun. The women not only learned to make healthy food, but they saw first hand that it was a lot of fun preparing food. It did my heart good to see them so happy!

Truly a "merry heart does good like a medicine" and I thank the Lord for sending Linda, Brenda, and Cinda to my country. God used them not only to teach our people how to eat healthfully but also how to have a joyful heart!

These three sisters have personally enriched my own life for to know them is to love them. Their love for Jesus shines brightly in everything they do. I am so excited about this cookbook because I have tasted many of their recipes.

Reading this book and cooking the recipes from it will be a most rewarding experience for you. It will help you become happier cooks, whose food will not only be nutritious, beautiful, and tasty, but also mixed with love and blessings for your family.

Julia Outkina

Julia Outkina
Director, Russian Branch of 3ABN

Tribute to Mom

Making our home happy and full of love was always a top priority with Mom.
With five children, this was no easy task, so Mom turned to God for help.
Daily, as she gathered her children around her, God rewarded her with patience,
energy, wisdom, and a song in her heart.

Mom instilled in her daughters as well as her sons the importance of preparing
nutritious meals for the family. She also felt the importance of everyone in the family
enjoying the meals together. We would share the day's events, laugh,
and just have fun. We looked forward to meal times and still do.

Mom, you are our favorite cook, and we dedicate our first cookbook to you.
Thank you for caring enough to give us a rich heritage of family love, fun,
and laughter but most of all for making Jesus first in your life and in our home.
Truly Proverbs 31:28 expresses the sentiments of our hearts, for we rise up
and call you blessed.

Acknowledgments

We would like to express our heartfelt thanks to all those who have helped to make *Cooking With the Micheff Sisters* possible.

We are very grateful to Three Angels Broadcasting Network—specifically Danny and Linda Shelton—for their loving support, invitations to tape cooking programs, and encouragement to share God's love through children's ministries. We especially want to thank Linda Shelton, our adopted sister, for her prayers and willing heart to share with others the abundant life. We love you, Linda.

We particularly want to thank our husbands for their willingness to taste our endless recipes. Their honest opinions and ideas make them great food critics. But most of all we want to thank Jim, Tim, and Joel for their unselfish love and their support for all the ministries we are involved in. We love you guys!

We have always enjoyed our family's scrumptious recipes and are delighted that we can share some of them with you. We want to thank Dad; Mom; our brother Ken and his wife Tammy; our brother Jim's wife, Gail; Cinda's daughter Catie; and Linda's mother-in-law, Aggie Johnson, for sharing some of their favorite recipes.

We want to thank our special friend Tammy Larson for being our photographer. She always wears a smile and never gives up until she gets it right. We appreciate the creative talents God has blessed her with and her willingness to share them with others.

We also want to thank Pacific Press, our publisher, for their many hours of hard work to make this cookbook possible: Susan Harvey, for her vision and enthusiasm; Tim Lale, for his many hours of hard work, support, and direction; Aileen Andres Sox, for her countless hours editing the recipes; and Michelle Petz for doing such a beautiful job on our cookbook's design and cover.

Most of all we want to thank our awesome God for always encouraging us to share His love with others.

Table of Contents

Introduction

Our parents made the decision to quit eating meat when we were very young. They had just come to know Jesus and were excited about following the healthy lifestyle that is outlined for us in the Bible—eating fruits, nuts, vegetables, and grains. They also wanted something better for their children than the poor health our grandparents had suffered from. Our parents believed that eating right would help keep us well and thus prevent expensive doctor's bills that they would have been hard-pressed to pay.

Mom believed that it was her sacred duty to learn to prepare healthy food for her family. She had never been taught to fix healthy foods, so with much prayer she began to develop recipes that tasted good and were nutritious too. We were very poor, so this was quite a challenge for Mom. Sometimes the only ingredients she had to work with were cornmeal and dried beans. She spent many hours in the kitchen with her children around her, teaching them what she was learning about preparing nutritious food on a limited income. She made this learning time a fun time, and God blessed her efforts.

Now that we are older we can see for ourselves the value of a healthy lifestyle. We also appreciate the decision our parents made so long ago to change our family's eating habits.

If you would like a lifestyle change, be assured that you have a heavenly Father who will help you. It is His desire and ours that above all things you prosper and be in good health (3 John 1:2). We pray that the recipes in this cookbook will be a blessing to you and your family.

With His blessings,

Linda, Brenda, and Cinda,

the Micheff sisters

Substitutions

Listed below are some of the substitutes for animal foods that we use in our recipes.

DAIRY SUBSTITUTES

Soy Good is one of Brenda and Linda's favorite soy milks. Plain and Simple is good for soups and gravies and over breakfast cereals. Regular Soy Good has a green label and good for anything that requires a sweeter taste. We love this brand because it does not have the strong aftertaste associated with some soy milk. You may substitute with your favorite brand.

Better Than Milk original flavor is great to cook with, on cold cereals, and for any recipe that calls for milk. Vanilla flavor is good for cookies, cakes, and baked goods. Neither of these products have a strong aftertaste. You may substitute with your favorite brand.

Nondairy whipped topping is a dairy-free substitute for whipped cream that can be found in most grocery stores and any natural food store. Use any brand you wish.

Tofutti Better Than Cream Cheese is similar in taste and texture to traditional cream cheese, but is milk- and butterfat-free and contains no cholesterol. It comes in 8-ounce containers and is available in ten different flavors. It is great in entrees, desserts, or as a spread for bagels. You can use this whenever a recipe calls for cream cheese.

Tofutti Sour Supreme or Better Than Sour Cream looks and tastes similar to dairy sour cream but is milk- and butterfat-free and contains no cholesterol. Sour Supreme has some trans fats, but is best for baking. Better Than Sour Cream has no trans fats, but does not work well for baking.

NATURAL SWEETENERS

Florida Crystals Milled Cane Sugar measures cup for cup like white sugar. There are no meat products used in processing.

Pure maple syrup is an all-natural product that can be used in many recipes as a substitute for granulated sugar. It is less expensive if purchased at large membership stores. It is also available in most local grocery stores.

Frozen 100 percent fruit juices are all-natural sweeteners. We use apple juice most frequently because its flavor does not overwhelm your recipe or change the color.

Sucanat Granulated Cane Juice by Wholesome Foods is an organic evaporated sugar cane juice with black strap molasses added to it. It replaces brown and white sugar cup for cup.

TOFU

Tofu is an excellent source of protein and contains no cholesterol. It also is an inexpensive substitute for meat, fish, poultry, and cheese.

Silken tofu is a soybean product with a silky smooth texture. It is great for cheesecakes, pies, puddings, and salad dressings.

Water-packed tofu comes in soft, firm, or extra-firm. It has to be refrigerated and has a shorter "shelf life." All water-packed tofus have a firmer spongier texture than silken and are good for foods such as mock scrambled eggs. Water-packed tofu can be crumbled, blended until smooth, sliced, baked, or boiled—the ideas are endless.

Mori-Nu Tofu does have to be refrigerated until opened and has a long shelf life. This product is great for making entrees, desserts, salad dressings, mock egg salad, and many other dishes.

Mori-Nu Mates are lemon- or vanilla-flavored substitutes for pudding mix. Mori-Nu Mates can be found in the health food section of larger grocery stores.

OTHER PRODUCTS

Follow Your Heart Vegenaise or Grapeseed Oil Vegenaise is a mayonnaise replacement. Grapeseed oil is an excellent natural source of vitamin E and essential fatty acids necessary for normal cell metabolism and maintenance. Vegenaise is found only in the refrigerated sections of grocery stores.

Carob chips are an alternative to chocolate chips. Some carob chips have dairy and lots of sweeteners in them. Co-ops and health food stores carry vegan carob chip sweetened with barley malt.

Liquid Aminos by Bragg is an unfermented soy sauce replacement made from soy protein. It can be used in entrees, Oriental foods, in marinades, gravies, and in any recipe that calls for soy sauce.

Vegex is an all-vegetable, beef-flavored seasoning that comes in a paste made from an extract of nutritional yeast (often called brewer's yeast). You can use it in soups, stews, broths, gravies, or any recipe in which you desire a beefy taste. If you can't find this product you can use vegetarian beef bouillon, which comes in dehydrated cubes, paste, or powder.

Pickapeppa Hot Sauce is made in Jamaica, with red Jamaican peppers. You can use your favorite brand of hot sauce if you can't find this one.

Scotch Bonnet Pepper Sauce is a very hot pepper concentrate. You can substitute your favorite brand of hot pepper sauce.

Nutritional Yeast Flakes (often called brewers yeast flakes) are a powerful source of B vitamins, amino acids, proteins, minerals, enzymes, and nucleic acids. This premium yeast is grown on sugar beets, which are known to absorb nutrients from the soil faster than almost any other crop. As a result, this yeast is exceptionally rich in selenium, chromium, potassium, copper, manganese, iron, zinc, and other nutrients natural to yeast. It is also gluten-free. This yeast can be used in entrees, as breading meal, or sprinkled on top of foods like popcorn and tofu scrambled eggs.

Good Seasons Italian Dressing Mix is a tasty salad dressing when mixed with olive oil; it also has a wonderful blend of seasonings that make it useful in many recipes. It is one of Brenda's "secret" ingredients. It is readily available in most grocery stores in the United States. If you can't find it, you can use a mix of the following ingredients as substitutes: onion powder, garlic powder, or garlic salt, red peppers, basil, oregano, thyme, salt, and parsley. Use amounts according to taste.

Rumford's Baking Powder is aluminum-free. Substitute any aluminum-free baking powder of your choice.

Egg replacer is found in your larger grocery stores. Cornstarch also works well as an egg replacer. Use one tablespoon of cornstarch for each egg in the recipe.

Soy margarine can usually be found in grocery or health food stores. Look for a brand that is vegan, nonhydrogenated, without trans-fats or cholesterol.

Pecan meal can usually be found in larger grocery stores or health food stores. Or you can make your own by grinding pecans in a food processor.

Dressler's Soy Add-Ums is an unflavored, dry, textured soy protein, made from defatted soy flour, which makes it easier to digest without gassy aftereffects! When hydrated and flavored, Soy Add-ums has the excellent "mouth feel" of a soft chewy meat with no aftertaste. This product takes on whatever flavor you add. It is inexpensive and can be used in any recipe that calls for beef: barbecue, sweet and sour chicken, chili, sloppy Joes, and stew, just to name a few! My (Brenda's) husband recently became a vegetarian, but he often dislikes soy products because of the taste and texture. He loves the Sloppy Joes (recipe on p. 68) I make with Soy Add-Ums and was shocked to learn that I hadn't used real meat!

Soy cheese is casein- and milk-free. We like the Tofutti brand best.

Yves Ground Round Veggie Original is a soy protein product that is fat-, cholesterol-, and preservative-free. It is precooked so all you do is heat and serve. This product can be used in any recipe that calls for ground hamburger. Meat eaters have told us that this product's texture most resembles real hamburger. Yves also has a whole line of other products available most of which are no fat or low fat! Their "Veggie Dogs" taste delicious and are fat-free!

Vege-Sal can be found in your local health food stores or in larger grocery stores. You can substitute with your favorite seasoned salt.

Fruit-sweetened catsup can be found in health food stores or in the health food section of larger grocery stores. One good product is Westbrae Natural Fruit Sweetened Catsup.

Appetizers

Eggplant Dip
p. 21

Hummus
p. 22

Stuffed Cherry Tomatoes
p. 26

Sesame
Bread Sticks
p. 17

Spinach-
Mushroom
Tarts   p. 28

Bruschetta
p. 16

Mushroom
Pinwheels
p. 25

Bruschetta

10 to 12 medium-size fresh tomatoes, peeled and diced

3 cloves garlic, peeled and crushed

½ cup chopped fresh basil (to taste)

Salt to taste

2 tablespoons extra virgin olive oil

1 loaf French or Italian bread, sliced

Mix together tomatoes, garlic, basil, and salt. Set aside approximately one hour before serving. Brush sliced bread with olive oil. Grill bread in a hot skillet or under a broiler until golden. Spoon tomato topping mounded over grilled bread.

You can also use the tomato topping for a main dish. Instead of serving on top of bread, try pouring it over hot pasta! It is delicious! I especially like it over angel hair or penne pasta. —Cinda

Yields 12 slices.

Per slice: Cal. 129 Fat 3.7g Sat. fat 0.6g Sod. 358mg Carb. 21.6g Diet. Fiber 1.4g Prot. 3.7g

Sesame Bread Sticks

Mix all ingredients except for the sesame seeds. Knead until dough is very smooth, elastic, and forms a ball. Add flour occasionally while kneading to prevent sticking. Cover the dough with a damp dish towel and let rest for about 5 minutes. Flour your hands and pat the dough into a rectangle on a well-floured work surface. With a rolling pin, roll the dough to a 16 x 6-inch rectangle, rolling evenly so that the bread sticks will be uniform in thickness. Brush the dough lightly with olive oil. Cover the dough with the damp dish towel and let rise until doubled, 1 to 1½ hours.

Toast sesame seeds by placing in a heavy dry skillet and stirring over medium heat until seeds are light golden, about 6 minutes. Set aside.

When dough has risen, heat oven to 425 degrees. Spray three baking sheets with a nonstick cooking spray or brush with small amount of olive oil. Lightly brush the dough with water. Sprinkle the dough with toasted sesame seeds, and press them down gently in the dough. With a chef's knife, cut the dough into 32 strips, each about ½-inch wide. Stretch one strip of dough to slightly less than width of the baking sheet and place it on the sheet, letting the dough come just to the edges. Stretch remaining strips, arranging them ¾-inch apart. Bake in the preheated oven (no more than two baking sheets at a time) until golden and crisp, 15 to 18 minutes. Transfer to wire rack. Cool completely.

Keep the unbaked bread sticks in the refrigerator until there is room in the oven to bake them.

Make spiral bread sticks by placing the strips of dough on the baking sheet and holding down one end with one hand while gently twisting the other end until you get a spiral effect. Then press both ends to the baking sheet so you won't lose the spiral. Bake as directed. These are wonderful as an appetizer with just about any dip. I also like to serve these at lunch or dinner in a bread basket along with other breads. —**Brenda**

Yields 32 bread sticks

3 to 3½ cups flour
1 tablespoon honey
1 teaspoon salt
2 packages instant
   dry yeast
¼ cup hot water
Toasted sesame seeds

Per bread stick: Cal. 72 Fat 1.9g Sat. fat 0.3g Sod. 70.6mg Carb. 12g Diet. Fiber 1g Prot. 2.2

Apple Crunch With Cinnamon Crisps

CINNAMON CRISPS:

6 flour tortillas

3 tablespoons Florida Crystals Milled Cane Sugar

1½ teaspoons cinnamon

APPLE CRUNCH:

4 cups finely chopped tart apples

½ cup quartered seedless red grapes

½ cup chopped celery

¼ cup chopped walnuts

3 tablespoons orange juice

1 tablespoon Florida Crystals Milled Cane Sugar

2 teaspoons grated orange peel

Coat both sides of each tortilla with nonstick cooking spray. Combine sugar and cinnamon; sprinkle over both sides of tortillas. Cut each into eight wedges. Place on baking sheets. Bake at 400 degrees for 4 to 5 minutes or until crisp. Watch carefully so they don't burn.

For apple crunch: While tortillas are baking, combine the apple crunch ingredients in a bowl. Serve with the cinnamon crisps.

This is wonderful as an appetizer or a healthy snack. The different textures of the fruits and nuts blend together to create a delicious treat. —**Cinda**

Yields 48 crisps

Per crisp: Cal. 43   Fat 1.1g   Sat. fat 0.2g   Sod. 43.7mg   Carb. 7.9g   Diet. Fiber 0.6g   Prot. 0.9g

Apple Dip

Mix ingredients together and serve with apple wedges.
Store in the refrigerator.

1 8-ounce container
Tofutti Better
Than Cream
Cheese

1 cup peanut butter

1 cup Sucanat
Granulated
Cane Juice

¼ cup prepared Better
Than Milk soy
milk, original
flavor

Children and adults alike love this one! You can use the leftovers in sandwiches—if there are any! —**Cinda**

Yields 12 ¹/₄-cup servings

Per serving: Cal. 197   Fat 16.7g   Sat. fat 3.6g   Sod. 207mg   Carb. 7.5g   Diet. Fiber 1.27g   Prot. 6.4g

Down Home Dilly Dip

Mix ingredients together. Serve with fresh vegetables and crackers.

1 8-ounce container
Tofutti Better
Than Sour
Cream

½ cup Grapeseed Oil
Vegenaise

2 tablespoons fresh
dill

¼ teaspoon Vege-Sal

2 tablespoons chives

This dip will keep in your refrigerator for several days. I have used this same recipe for my potato or macaroni salad, and it is delicious! —**Cinda**

Yields 8 to 10 2-tablespoon servings

Per serving: Cal. 110   Fat 11.1g   Sat. fat 2.8g   Sod. 195mg   Carb. 1.6g   Diet. Fiber 0g   Prot. 0.8g

Apricot Chutney Spread

1 8-ounce package Tofutti Better Than Cream Cheese

½ cup dried apricots, chopped fine

2 scallions, minced

¼ teaspoon ground ginger

¼ teaspoon salt

½ cup apricot (or plain) chutney

Sesame crackers

In a medium bowl, combine Better Than Cream Cheese, dried apricots, scallions, ginger, and salt. Set aside.

Remove fruit from chutney and chop fine. Add chopped fruit and chutney syrup to cheese mixture. Mix all ingredients until blended. Chill in refrigerator at least 8 hours. Serve with sesame crackers or cracker of your choice.

This recipe can be changed easily by exchanging the apricots for any other dried fruit, such as raisins, prunes, or cherries. I happen to love apricots but have liked the other fruits too! —**Brenda**

Yields 8 to 10 2-tablespoon servings

Per serving: Cal. 76   Fat 6.4g   Sat. fat 1.6g   Sod. 164mg   Carb. 3.9g   Diet. Fiber 0.4g   Prot. 1g

Eggplant Dip

In a large skillet, heat the 4 tablespoons olive oil. Sauté eggplant until golden brown. Remove from heat and set aside. Add remaining 2 tablespoons of olive oil to skillet. Sauté garlic, celery, and red pepper. Stir in eggplant, tomato sauce, cayenne, cumin, cane sugar, salt, and apple cider vinegar. Cover and simmer 15 minutes. Uncover and simmer 20 minutes longer. Chill dip 6 to 8 hours.

Just before serving, stir in parsley. Serve at room temperature with cracker bread, crackers, or pita bread.

This is a wonderful dip to serve when you are having an appetizer buffet. No last minute stress because you make it ahead of time. And, since it is best at room temperature, you don't have to worry about keeping it hot or making sure it stays chilled! —Cinda

4 tablespoons plus 2 tablespoons olive oil

1 large eggplant, peeled and cut into ½-inch cubes

1 clove garlic, crushed

1 cup diced celery

1 red sweet pepper, chopped

1 8-ounce can tomato sauce

¼ teaspoon cayenne

1 tablespoon cumin

2 tablespoons Florida Crystals Milled Cane Sugar

2 teaspoons salt

¼ cup apple cider vinegar

2 teaspoons salt

¼ cup chopped parsley

Yields 8 to 10 ¼-cup servings

Per serving: Cal. 127   Fat 10.7g   Sat. fat 1.3g   Sod. 181mg   Carb. 7.5g   Diet. Fiber 1.9g   Prot. 2.3g

Guacamole Dip

2 large ripe avocados, halved and peeled

1 medium tomato, diced

Juice of 1 lemon

Garlic salt to taste

Salt to taste

Place avocados in a small bowl. Mash with a fork. (May use food processor if careful to not overprocess.) Add remaining ingredients and mix well. Serve with tortilla chips or crispy baked pita wedges.

If you love avocados, you are going to love this dip. And it is so easy to make! Don't make it too far ahead of time, though, because it does have a tendency to turn dark quickly. Try substituting 1/2 cup salsa for the fresh tomato. This gives the guacamole a spicier flavor and is also delicious. —**Brenda**

Yields 16 2-tablespoon servings

Per serving: Cal. 30 Fat 2.2g Sat. fat 0.4g Sod. 139mg Carb. 2.9g Diet. Fiber 1.4g Prot. 0.5g

Hummus

3 16-ounce cans chickpeas*

2 teaspoons minced garlic

3 tablespoons lemon juice

¾ cup roasted tahini

¼ cup olive oil or 2 tablespoons olive oil + 2 tablespoons chickpea juice

1 teaspoon salt (to taste)

1 cup chopped walnuts

Sliced black olives, paprika, and fresh parsley for garnish

Combine all ingredients except garnishes in a large bowl. Purée in batches in food processor or blender until smooth. Keep refrigerated until serving. Garnish with black olives, paprika, and fresh parsley.

Hummus can be used as a sandwich spread or vegetable dip. It also freezes well.

*Also called garbanzo beans or ceci beans.

I had an Egyptian-theme birthday party for my husband and served bowls of this dip along with pita bread cut into triangles. The guests loved munching on this as they visited and awaited the main course. —**Cinda**

Yields 40 servings

Per serving: Cal. 78 Fat 5.7g Sat. fat 0.7g Sod. 114mg Carb. 5.7g Diet. Fiber 1.3g Prot. 2.7g

Veggie-Chili Dip

In a baking dish, layer ingredients in the order listed. Bake at 350 degrees until hot and bubbly. Serve hot with tortilla chips or toasted pita triangles.

This is one of those fast and easy recipes that I can put together at a moment's notice. My family loves it, and the best part is that it has only four ingredients! —Brenda

Yields 8 ¹/₄-cup servings

- 2 8-ounce containers Toffuti Better Than Cream Cheese
- 1 tablespoon chopped chives or green onions
- ¼ cup green chiles
- 2 16-ounce cans vegetarian chili

Per serving: Cal. 239   Fat 16.1g   Sat. fat 4g   Sod. 589mg   Carb. 16g   Diet. Fiber 3.7g   Prot. 7.6g

Elegant Potato Puffs

Mash hot potatoes with the Better Than Cream Cheese until creamy. Add salt to taste. Roll out one puff pastry sheet. Spread potato mixture on top of sheet. Roll up and cut into thick slices. Place on a cookie sheet. Repeat with rest of puff pastry sheets. Bake at 400 degrees for 15 to 25 minutes or until golden brown. Serve hot.

I love these puffs! They combine two of my favorite foods—potatoes and pastry! They can also be made ahead of time and frozen either baked or unbaked. Thaw and then bake or warm to serve. —Cinda

Yields 12 puffs

- 5 large potatoes, peeled and boiled until tender
- 1 8-ounce container herb and chive flavor Tofutti Better Than Cream Cheese
- Salt to taste
- 1 17¼-ounce package frozen puff pastry sheets

Per serving: Cal. 497   Fat 21.7g   Sat. fat 3.7g   Sod. 220mg   Carb. 69g   Diet. Fiber 4.3g   Prot. 7.1g

Florentine-Artichoke Gratin

1 medium onion, chopped

2 garlic cloves, minced

Olive oil

1 8-ounce container Tofutti Better Than Cream Cheese

6 cups coarsely chopped fresh spinach

2 13½-ounce jars marinated artichoke hearts

½ cup Grapeseed Oil Vegenaise

1 8-ounce container Tofutti Sour Supreme

Salt to taste

Dash of cayenne (optional)

1 teaspoon fresh lemon juice

TOPPING:

1 cup toasted chopped pecans

2 cups herb-seasoned stuffing mix

3 tablespoons margarine

Sauté onion and garlic in small amount of olive oil until onions are translucent. Add Better Than Cream Cheese and stir until melted. Add rest of ingredients and stir until mixed. Spoon into a baking dish sprayed with a nonstick cooking spray.

For topping: On microwave-safe plate, spread pecans evenly. Microwave on high power for 2 minutes; stir. Continue microwaving on high, checking every 30 seconds, until nuts are fragrant and browned.

Mix topping ingredients together and spread over spinach mixture. Bake at 350 degrees for 20 to 30 minutes or until bubbly. Serve hot with crackers, bread, or pita triangles. May also be used as a side dish.

This dish is a favorite at all my parties. I even served it as a side dish at one of my luncheons! Everyone asked for the recipe! —**Cinda**

Yields 16 servings

Per serving: Cal. 314   Fat 19g   Sat. fat 4g   Sod. 833mg   Carb. 31g   Diet. Fiber 5g   Prot. 7g

Mushroom Pinwheels

Sauté onion in olive oil until onions are clear. Add mushrooms and cook till tender. Add salt and herbs. Cool slightly. Stir in Better Than Cream Cheese.

Roll out puff pastry sheets just slightly. Spread filling mixture over puff pastry sheets. Roll tightly. Slice into 1/2-inch rings and place on cookie sheet. Bake at 350 degrees 10 to 15 minutes, until golden.

This is a fun and easy recipe to make, and your guests will think you have spent hours working in the kitchen. Diced pimentos will add a little zing! I like to add them during the holidays just to add a festive touch of color! You can also make these ahead of time and freeze them. —**Brenda**

1 onion, finely minced

2 tablespoons olive oil

2 10-ounce packages fresh sliced mushrooms

Salt to taste

1 teaspoon thyme

1 teaspoon basil (optional)

1 8-ounce container Tofutti Better Than Cream Cheese

1 package puff pastry sheets

Yields 24 pinwheels

Per pinwheel: Cal. 71 Fat 5.8g Sat. fat 1.1g Sod. 150mg Carb. 4.4g Diet. Fiber 0.5g Prot. 1.2g

Olive-Pimento Roll-Ups

1 8-ounce container herb and chive flavor Tofutti Better Than Cream Cheese

½ cup chopped black olives

½ cup chopped pimentos

4 8-inch wheat flour tortillas

In medium bowl mix all ingredients (except tortillas) until blended. Spread mixture on tortilla and roll up tightly, jellyroll style. Cover with plastic wrap and chill for 2 to 3 hours. To serve, cut each roll-up crosswise into ½-inch slices to form pinwheels. Garnish with pimento strips.

Variations: Add to Better Than Cream Cheese mixture green chiles, scallions, green olives, or chopped walnuts.

I serve this quite frequently when I entertain, and it seems I can never make enough! But don't wait to have a party to try these. These are just as wonderful for a quiet dinner for two or feeding a family of six! Try different fillings for variety! —Brenda

Yields 56 roll-ups

Per roll-up: Cal. 23 Fat 1.5g Sat. fat 0.4g Sod. 41.9mg Carb. 2.2g Diet. Fiber 0.2g Prot. 0.5g

Stuffed Cherry Tomatoes

1 large ripe avocado

1 tablespoon Grapeseed Oil Vegenaise

2 tablespoons lemon juice

1 12.3-ounce package firm Mori-Nu Tofu

¾ teaspoon salt (to taste)

¼ teaspoon cayenne (optional)

36 cherry tomatoes (approximate)

1 bunch parsley

Halve and peel avocado and place in a small bowl. Mash with fork. Stir in Vegenaise and lemon juice. Add tofu and seasonings. Stir well. Gently score around the top of each tomato and hollow it out. Drain upside down on a paper towel for several minutes. Using a pastry bag or a small spoon, fill each tomato. (This can be done up to 8 hours ahead of time.) Serve on platter covered with fresh parsley.

This is not only colorful and pretty but easy to make as well. When I had my catering business, I made these for a party of 500 people. They must have loved them because they ate every one of them and asked if I had more! —Cinda

Yields 36 stuffed tomatoes; serves 10 to 12

Per serving: Cal. 64 Fat 3.4g Sat. fat 3.9g Sod. 227mg Carb. 4.5g Diet. Fiber 1.4g Prot. 4.8g

Stuffed Mushrooms

Clean mushrooms. Remove and save stems. Place caps open side up on a nonstick baking sheet or a baking sheet sprayed with nonstick cooking spray. Finely chop mushroom stems and set aside.

In olive oil, sauté onions until translucent. Add stems, cooking until tender. Add bread crumbs, pecans, and Stripples.

Dissolve bouillon cube in hot water and add to mixture. Mix until well blended and holding together. Add more water if needed. (Mixture should not be wet but should hold together firmly.) Place a heaping teaspoonful of mixture into each mushroom cap, spreading out to the edge. Bake at 350 degrees for 15 to 20 minutes until slightly crispy. Serve hot.

These are great not only for appetizers but for brunch, or even for your main meal. I especially like to fix these when I have guests for dinner, and I can tell you from experience, your meat-eating friends won't even miss the bacon! If you don't have Stripples, you can substitute imitation Baco-Bits. —**Brenda**

2 pounds large whole fresh mushrooms

2 tablespoons olive oil or margarine

½ cup finely diced onion

⅔ cup bread crumbs

1 tablespoon finely chopped pecans

3 Worthington Stripples bacon substitute, finely chopped

1 chicken-flavored bouillon cube

¼ cup hot water

Yields 50 stuffed mushrooms

Per mushroom: Cal. 14 Fat .9g Sat. fat 0.1g Sod. 29mg Carb. 1.39g Diet. Fiber 0.3g Prot. 0.5g

Spinach-Mushroom Tarts

2 tablespoons
  margarine

1 large onion, diced

1 10-ounce package
  fresh mushrooms,
  diced

2 10-ounce packages
  frozen chopped
  spinach, thawed
  but undrained

½ cup Wondra flour

2½ cups Better Than
  Milk soy milk

1 8-ounce container
  herb and chive
  flavor Tofutti
  Better Than
  Cream Cheese

48 ready-made pastry
  cups, baked

Grape tomatoes for
  garnish

In a skillet over medium heat, melt margarine. Sauté onion until translucent. Add diced fresh mushrooms; continue cooking until mushrooms are tender (about 4 minutes). Add thawed, undrained spinach.

Combine flour and soy milk in a shaker container. Shake until well mixed. Add to spinach mixture. Add the Better Than Cream Cheese and cook until completely melted. Scoop cooked mixture into pastry cups and serve warm. Garnish with a slice of a grape tomato.

This is a recipe that my girls enjoy making with me. We always have lots of fun in the kitchen, and they especially like filling the pastry shells and decorating the tops. I think anytime you include your children in the kitchen, you are not only teaching them to cook, you are also making wonderful memories. —Brenda

Yield 48 tarts

Per serving: Cal. 296   Fat 20.4g   Sat. fat 5.1g   Sod. 161mg   Carb. 24g   Diet. Fiber 1.3g   Prot. 4.6g

Hawaiian Sweet & Sour Meatballs

Purée onion and tofu in food processor. Pour into larger mixing bowl. Add all other ingredients except for the soy milk and sauce. Mix well. *(I use gloves and mix well with my hands.)*

Add soy milk a little at a time, until mixture sticks together.

Using a 1-inch scoop, place scoops of mixture onto cookie sheet that has been sprayed with a nonstick cooking spray. (If you do not have a 1-inch scoop, you may roll into bite-size balls.) Place in oven and bake at 350 degrees for approximately 30 minutes until slightly crispy.

Pour sauce (directions below) over balls and serve hot. The balls may be kept in a Crock-Pot on the lowest setting. (You do not want them to cook in the Crock-Pot because they will get soft and fall apart.) You can also put the baked balls into a casserole, cover with sauce, and bake them in the oven for 20 to 30 minutes until hot and sauce is bubbly.

For sauce: In a saucepan, mix together chili sauce and jellied cranberry sauce. Simmer until heated through, stirring with wire whisk until smooth. Add pineapple tidbits.

I made this recipe a little larger because I use it for entertaining guests. If you want to serve fewer people, just divide the recipe in half, or make the entire recipe and freeze half the balls for next time! I love to serve this recipe whenever I have meat-eating guests for dinner. That's because I have so much fun trying to convince them that these "meatballs" do not contain any meat. Sometimes I even have to go get the recipe to prove it to them! —**Brenda**

2 large onions

2 to 3 packages tofu, any style or brand

1 16-ounce bag stuffing mix

4 to 5 cups quick-cooking oats

2 cups crushed saltine crackers (fat-free if available)

2 cups chopped pecans (or any nuts)

2 packages Good Seasons Italian Dressing Mix

2 cups cooked lentils (optional)

2 cups cooked brown rice (optional)

Better Than Milk soy milk (just enough to moisten mixture)

Sauce (recipe below)

SAUCE:

2 12-ounce bottles chili sauce

2 16-ounce cans jellied cranberry sauce

1 16-ounce can pineapple tidbits

Yields 48 balls

Each meatball: Cal. 125 Fat 4g Sat. fat 1.5g Sod. 277mg Carb. 18g Diet. Fiber 1.7g Prot. 4g

Traveling Taco

1 14-ounce can refried beans

1 8-ounce container Tofutti Better Than Sour Cream

1 cup guacamole

¼ cup taco sauce

1 4.5-ounce can diced green chiles

2 scallions, chopped

1 medium tomato, diced

1 16-ounce can sliced black olives

Tomatoes and parsley for garnish

On a round serving platter, layer the ingredients in the order listed. Garnish with tomato roses.*

*To make a tomato rose, use a sharp knife to peel a thin strip, starting at the stem end, until all the skin is removed. Coil skin to form the shape of a rose. Place in the center of the Traveling Taco. Add a sprig of parsley on each side of your tomato rose.

I named this recipe "Traveling Taco" because whenever I am asked to bring something to a party, this one always travels with me! My girls think that it's not a party unless they have this special dish! —**Brenda**

Yields 12 to 14 2-tablespoon servings

Per serving: Cal. 107   Fat 6.8g   Sat. fat 1.8g   Sod. 295mg   Carb. 10g   Diet. Fiber 2.74g   Prot. 3.21g

Won Ton Vege-Sausage Cups

Preheat oven to 350 degrees. Mix together all ingredients except the won ton wrappers and set aside. Spray a mini muffin tin with a nonstick cooking spray of your choice. Lightly press one wrapper into each cup. Spray each wrapper with nonstick cooking spray and bake 5 minutes or until golden brown. Remove from tins and place on baking sheet. Fill with mixture and bake 5 to 10 minutes, until bubbly.

This is one of my dad's favorites. I always make it for my annual Christmas party. The filling can be made a couple of days ahead of time and refrigerated. The won tons can also be baked ahead of time and kept in an airtight container at room temperature. Right before your guests arrive, fill the won tons and bake. —Cinda

2 cups *crumbled* Worthington Prosage

1½ cups grated cheddar-style soy cheese

1½ cups grated Monterey Jack-style soy cheese

1 cup ranch dressing (prepared from a mix)

1 2.25-ounce can sliced black olives

½ cup chopped red pepper or pimentos

1 12-ounce package fresh or frozen won ton wrappers

Yields 48 to 50 won-ton cups

Per serving: Cal. 58 Fat 2.8g Sat. fat 0.2g Sod. 166mg Carb. 5.6g Diet. Fiber 0.3g Prot. 2.8g

Breakfast & Breads

Orange-Almond
Muffins
p. 38

Pancakes
p. 43

Scrambled
Tofu Burritos
p. 47

Maple
Nut Rolls
p. 36

Breakfast
Frittata
p. 48

Maple Nut Rolls

4 cups warm water

¾ cup canola oil

1 cup apple juice
    concentrate

½ cup applesauce

½ cup Sucanat
    Granulated
    Cane Juice

4 teaspoons salt

2 cups whole-wheat
    flour

5 pounds unbleached
    white flour

4 tablespoons yeast

2 recipes Date Jam
    (recipe below)

Cinnamon

Maple syrup

4 cups pecan halves
    (or other nuts)

DATE JAM:

4 cups dates

1 cup water

In a large bowl mix together water, oil, apple juice concentrate, applesauce, Sucanat, and salt. Add some of the flour. Add more flour alternately with the yeast. Keep adding flour until you have a soft dough. (For lighter dough, use three parts white flour to one part wheat.) Let rest approximately 20 minutes.

Stretch dough out on a flat surface until it is a rectangle about ½-inch thick. Spread with Date Jam (directions below). Sprinkle cinnamon on top of the date jam. Roll up dough and slice into 1½-inch slices.

Spray baking pan with nonstick cooking spray. Pour maple syrup in the bottom of the baking pan. Sprinkle pecan halves (or your favorite nuts) on top of the maple syrup. Place the cinnamon rolls about ½ inch apart in the pan. Let rise until double in size. Bake at 350 degrees for 25 to 30 minutes.

Flip the rolls upside down onto a platter immediately after removing them from the oven. Cool and serve with your favorite fruit salad.

For Date Jam: In a microwave-safe bowl, pour water over dates. Microwave on high 1 to 2 minutes. Put in blender and blend until very smooth. Add more water if mixture is too thick to blend. This jam is also great on toast.

These rolls make a delicious treat for Sabbath mornings. To reheat them, preheat your oven to 350. Sprinkle the top of the rolls with water and cover them with foil. Heat for 5 to 7 minutes. Serve with your favorite hot cereal and a fresh fruit salad. A gift of these rolls to friends or neighbors is a great way to let them know that they are special to you. —**Linda**

Makes 50 rolls

Each roll: Cal. 370   Fat 10.7g   Sat. fat 0.9g   Sod. 186mg   Carb. 62.5g   Diet. Fiber 5.8g   Prot. 10.4g

Date-Bran Muffins

Add baking soda to boiling water and stir. Set aside to cool.

In a large mixing bowl, combine oil, applesauce, and sweeteners. Blend well. Add egg replacer and mix again. Add baking soda mixture, soy milk, lemon juice, flour, salt, cereals, and dates. Mix well; allow to stand until dry ingredients absorb some liquid, about 5 minutes.

Spoon batter into muffin cups and bake for 25 minutes at 375 degrees.

I have included the amounts for making a larger batch because I like to make these muffins ahead of time and keep them in the freezer. They keep frozen approximately four weeks. I take a few out at a time as needed and let them come to room temperature. They are good just like this or heated in a microwave or oven. Don't microwave for more than 10 seconds because it will change the texture of the bread. —Cinda

ONE DOZEN MUFFINS

1½ teaspoons baking soda
½ cup boiling water
2 tablespoons oil
2 tablespoons thick applesauce
¼ cup Sucanat Granulated Cane Juice
¼ cup pure maple sugar
Egg replacer for 1 egg or 1 tablespoon cornstarch
1 cup soy milk
1 tablespoon lemon juice
1 cup flour
¼ teaspoon salt
1½ cups bran cereal, such as Bran Buds
½ cup bran flake cereal with raisins
½ cup uncooked seven-grain cereal
1 cup chopped dates

FIVE DOZEN MUFFINS

5 teaspoons baking soda
2 cups boiling water
½ cup oil
½ cup thick applesauce
1 cup Sucanat Granulated Cane Juice
1 cup pure maple sugar
Egg replacer for 4 eggs or 4 tablespoons cornstarch
1 quart soy milk
¼ cup lemon juice
4 cups flour
1 teaspoon salt
4 cups bran cereal, such as Bran Buds
2 cups bran flake cereal with raisins
2 cups uncooked seven-grain cereal
3 cups chopped dates

Per muffin: Cal. 172 Fat 3.4g Sat. fat 0.3g Sod. 328mg Carb. 36g Diet. Fiber 6.5g Prot. 4g

Orange-Almond Muffins

1½ cups unbleached white flour

½ cup whole-wheat pastry flour

1 tablespoon Rumford's Baking Powder

½ cup soy milk powder

1/8 teaspoon cinnamon

½ teaspoon salt

½ cup canola oil

1 teaspoon vanilla

¼ cup pure maple syrup

1 teaspoon grated orange rind

1½ cups orange juice

¼ cup almonds (to taste)

In a large mixing bowl, mix the dry ingredients together and make a well in the middle of the ingredients. Pour the oil, vanilla, pure maple syrup, orange rind, and orange juice in the middle of the dry ingredients. Stir gently until combined.

Spray muffin pan with nonstick cooking spray. Fill each muffin cup three quarters full of batter. Sprinkle sliced almonds on top of each muffin.

Bake at 350 degrees for 20 to 25 minutes until done. Check doneness by inserting a toothpick in the middle of the muffin. If it comes out clean, the muffin is baked.

Variations: Omit the orange juice and orange rind. In its place add your favorite all-fruit juice and ¼ cup of diced fruit. Instead of nuts on top of the muffin, spoon ½ teaspoon of all-fruit jam on top of each muffin and bake. Enjoy! —Linda

Makes 12 muffins

Per muffin: Cal. 264 Fat 12.6g Sat. fat 0.9g Sod. 182.5mg Carb. 40g Diet. Fiber 1.3g Prot. 4.8g

No Shortening Biscuits

Stir the dry ingredients together in a large mixing bowl. Pour in the oil. Cut it in with a pastry blender or two butter knives until mixture is "pebbly" in texture. Gradually stir in the soy milk. Stop adding the soy milk when the mixture separates from the sides of the bowl and forms a ball.

Roll the dough out on a floured surface and cut into biscuits.

Bake on a cookie sheet at 425 degrees for about 10 minutes, or until golden brown on the outside and slightly doughy on the inside. Serve warm.

1½ cups unbleached flour

½ cup whole wheat pastry flour

1 tablespoon Rumford's Baking Powder

½ teaspoon salt

¼ cup canola oil or light olive oil

6 to 8 ounces soy milk

My family loves biscuits, so they were excited that I came up with a healthy recipe for them. The biscuits are also good as a side for stews or any thick soup, and even can be the bread for small sandwiches. —**Cinda**

Makes 6 to 12 biscuits

Per serving: Cal. 216 Fat 7.7g Sat. fat 0.4g Sod. 252mg Carb. 38.4g Diet. Fiber 1.1g Prot. 6.2g

Pita Pocket Bread

4½ to 4¾ cups
    unbleached white
    flour or whole-
    wheat flour

1 package instant dry
    yeast

1½ teaspoons Florida
    Crystals Milled
    Cane Sugar

1½ teaspoons salt

1¾ cups water

2 tablespoons oil

In a large bowl, add 2 cups of the flour, yeast, sugar, and salt. Mix well.

In medium saucepan over medium heat, heat water and oil until warm (120 to 130 degrees). Add to flour mixture. With a hand mixer, mix at low speed until moistened. Gradually mix in enough flour to make dough firm. Knead on floured surface until smooth and elastic. Cover dough with plastic wrap and a towel. Let rest 20 minutes.

Punch down dough. Divide into twelve equal parts. Shape each part into a smooth ball. Place on board an inch apart. Cover and let rise 30 minutes.

Preheat oven to 500 degrees. Roll each ball into a 6-inch circle. Place three circles at a time, making sure they do not touch, directly onto oven rack. Bake about three minutes, until puffed and top just begins to brown. Cool on racks.

Cut in half and add filling of your choice.

These pita pockets are great with a hummus spread inside with lettuce, tomato, avocado, and cucumbers. You can also fill them with peanut butter and jam, vegetarian luncheon meat slices, or vege-burgers. I have served these pocket breads filled with wild rice, sliced fresh tomatoes, and lettuce, and it is absolutely delicious! I recommend them served plain with Indian food. Be creative and put your favorite sandwich filling inside! —**Brenda**

Yields 12 pitas

Per pita: Cal. 194   Fat 2.8g   Sat. fat 0.2g   Sod. 1.2mg   Carb. 36.4g   Diet. Fiber 1.4g   Prot. 5g

Whole-Wheat Bread

In the bowl of an extra-heavy-duty mixer, add water, apple juice concentrate, salt, oil, applesauce, and oatmeal. Blend together flour, yeast, and gluten flour. Slowly add flour mixture to wet ingredients until it makes soft dough that does not stick to your hands. (It will take about 5 pounds of finely ground whole-wheat flour.) Mix approximately 15 minutes.

Place dough on a flat surface. Cover with a clean dishcloth and let it rise until it doubles in size.

Divide dough into seven pieces. Knead and shape into loaves. Place in bread pans that have been sprayed with a nonstick cooking spray. Place bread pans in a warm place. (I put mine on top of my stove.) Let rise until loaves are double in size.

Place loaves in 350-degree oven and bake for 30 minutes, or until golden brown. Remove loaves from pans and place on a cooling rack. Serve with your favorite jam.

Sometimes instead of oatmeal I use whatever hot cereal we have had for breakfast. Seven-grain cereal gives it a great taste. I sometimes add raisins and nuts. —**Linda**

4 cups warm water

1 cup apple juice concentrate

4 scant teaspoons salt

¾ cup oil

1 cup applesauce

1 cup cooked oatmeal

8 cups flour (approximately)

4 tablespoons active dry yeast

4 tablespoons *gluten flour*

Yields 7 loaves

Per loaf: Cal. 798   Fat 27.6g   Sat. fat 2g   Sod. 1320mg   Carb. 123g   Diet. Fiber 18.6g   Prot. 25g

Brenda's Breakfast Bread

4 cups very warm water (120 to 130 degrees)

⅔ cup canola oil

1 tablespoon salt

⅔ cup honey

1 cup cooked oatmeal

½ cup molasses

1 cup white flour

3 cups plus 5 to 7 cups whole-wheat flour, as needed

4 tablespoons active dry yeast

1 cup chopped apricots

1 cup chopped dates

1 cup raisins

1 cup chopped prunes

1 cup chopped pecans

In a large mixing bowl, place very warm water, oil, salt, honey, oatmeal, molasses, white flour, and 3 cups whole-wheat flour. Mix together, and then add yeast. Continue adding flour until a thick dough is formed.

Place dough on floured flat surface and knead 10 to 15 minutes until smooth and elastic. Spray mixing bowl with a nonstick cooking spray and place dough in bowl. Cover and let rise 20 to 30 minutes in a warm place* until double in size.

Punch down and let rise again. When size of dough has doubled the second time, punch down and add all the dried fruit and nuts, kneading into dough. Divide dough into five equal parts. Shape into five loaves. Place each into a 5 x 9-inch bread pan and into a cool oven. Shut the door and let rise until double in size.

While bread is still inside the oven, turn oven to 350 degrees and bake for 30 minutes. Cool on racks.

*I usually put the dough in a cold oven and turn on the oven light. The light makes the oven just warm enough.

This bread freezes very well. Be sure to use thick freezer bags to prevent freezer burn. Serve for breakfast either plain or toasted. In fact, you don't have to wait until breakfast to enjoy it. Eat it anytime! —**Brenda**

Yields 6 loaves

Per loaf: Cal. 759   Fat 38g   Sat. fat 3g   Sod. 446mg   Carb. 105g   Diet. Fiber 8.6g   Prot. 8g

Mix all ingredients together. Pour about 1/4 cup batter onto hot griddle for each pancake. When pancakes start to bubble, flip and cook until golden. Serve hot with your favorite fruit topping or pure maple syrup!

Use less batter for smaller pancakes. —**Brenda**

1 cup all-purpose flour (or half white and half whole-wheat)

2 teaspoons Rumford's Baking Powder

1 teaspoon baking soda

1 tablespoon oil

1 teaspoon Florida Crystals Milled Cane Sugar

1/2 teaspoon salt

1 cup soy milk

1 tablespoon cornstarch

1 teaspoon vanilla

Yields six 6-inch pancakes

Per pancake: Cal. 119   Fat 3.3g   Sat. fat 0.3g   Sod. 780mg   Carb. 19g   Diet. Fiber 1g   Prot. 3g

Soy Crepes

1 cup whole-wheat
    pastry flour

1 cup unbleached
    white flour

1 teaspoon Rumford's
    Baking Powder

½ teaspoon salt

⅓ cup soy milk
    powder

3 tablespoons
    unsweetened
    applesauce

3 cups water

Fruit filling
    (recipe below)

FRUIT FILLING:

4 to 6 cups fresh
    strawberries

1 12-ounce can apple
    juice concentrate

¼ cup cornstarch

¼ cup cold water

Combine all ingredients and beat well by hand. Let batter sit for about 10 minutes.

Heat a 9-inch skillet and spray with a nonstick cooking spray. Pour ¼ cup of batter into pan and immediately tilt and rotate pan so that batter forms an even layer over the whole bottom. Cook over medium-high heat until the top starts to dry and the edges loosen. Slide pancake turner under the crepe, flip over, and cook the other side. Cool on wire rack.

For the fruit filling: Slice fresh strawberries into a bowl and set aside. Heat apple juice concentrate in a saucepan and bring to a boil. Mix cornstarch with cold water. Using a wire whisk, stir into boiling juice. Stir until thickened. Pour gently over berries and fold into crepes.

Put fruit filling in the crepe and roll it up. Top with nondairy whipped topping and fresh fruit. —Linda

Yields 10 to 12 8-inch crepes

Per crepe, including filling: Cal. 158 Fat 1g Sat. fat 0.1g Sod. 154mg Carb. 35.6g Diet. Fiber 2.6g Prot. 3g

Pumpkin Bread

In a large mixing bowl, sift dry ingredients together. Make a hole in the center of the dry ingredients and add remaining ingredients. Mix until smooth. Bake in 4 small loaf pans at 350 degrees approximately 45 minutes or 2 large loaf pans at 350 degrees for 1 hour. Bread is done when a toothpick inserted in center comes out clean.

Using a dark pan will shorten baking time. —Brenda

3½ cups flour

2½ cups Florida Crystals Milled Cane Sugar

3 teaspoons nutmeg

1 cup canola oil

2 teaspoons baking soda

4 tablespoons cornstarch

3 teaspoons cinnamon

2 cups pumpkin

1 teaspoon salt

⅔ cup water

½ teaspoon cloves

½ cup raisins

½ cup chopped pecans

Each large loaf yields 16 slices

Per large loaf slice: Cal. 198   Fat 8.5g   Sat. fat 0.7g   Sod. 208mg   Carb. 30g   Diet. Fiber 1.3g   Prot. 1.8g

Corn Bread

1 cup flour

¾ cup cornmeal

¼ cup Florida
    Crystals Milled
    Cane Sugar

¾ teaspoon salt

3 teaspoons baking
    powder

1 cup soy milk

1 tablespoon
    cornstarch

2 tablespoons canola
    oil

Mix all ingredients together and pour into a greased 8 x 8-inch or 9 x 9-inch glass baking dish. Bake 25 to 30 minutes at 350 degrees until golden. Serve hot!

This corn bread is wonderful served with chili or any hot soup! —**Brenda**

Yields 9 pieces

Per serving: Cal. 286 Fat 8.5g Sat. 0.5g Sod. 381mg Carb. 45.6g Diet. Fiber 1.2g Prot. 10.5g

Baco-Chip Gravy

¾ cup Wondra flour
    or all-purpose
    flour

3 cups soy milk

1 teaspoon salt

¼ cup imitation
    bacon bits

Mix flour, soy milk, and salt well and pour into a sauce pan. Heat over medium heat; stir constantly until thickened. (This will only take a couple of minutes.) Add imitation bacon bits and serve immediately.

This gravy is great served over biscuits or toast. I serve it for breakfast, brunch, or a light supper. It is fast and easy to make. —**Cinda**

Yields 14 ¼-cup servings

Per serving: Cal. 67 Fat 2.6g Sat. fat 0.4g Sod. 269mg Carb. 7.7g Diet. Fiber 1.4g Prot. 3.9g

Scrambled Tofu Burritos

Crumble both kinds of tofu into a mixing bowl. Add yeast, seasonings, and green chiles and set aside.

Sauté 1 cup chopped green onion in water until water is gone. Mix in seasoned tofu and simmer for approximately 15 to 20 minutes.

Serve wrapped in flour tortillas with your favorite toppings.

I love to serve these burritos for a brunch, especially when I have a lot of guests. I serve buffet-style, letting the guests make their own burritos. Add a potato dish and fresh fruit to complete the menu! —**Cinda**

1 pound firm, water-packed tofu, rinsed and drained

1 12.3-ounce package Mori-Nu Tofu, firm or extra-firm

¼ cup nutritional yeast

1½ tablespoons chicken-like seasoning

2 teaspoons beef-like seasoning

1 teaspoon Vege-Sal, optional

¼ teaspoon garlic powder

1 4.5-ounce can diced green chiles

1 cup chopped green onions

¼ cup water

10 flour tortillas

Topping suggestions:

Tofutti Better Than Sour Cream; diced fresh tomatoes; guacamole; tofu cheese; salsa; sliced black olives; shredded lettuce

Yields 10 burritos

Per burrito without toppings: Cal. 267   Fat 5g   Sat. fat 1.6g   Sod. 624mg   Carb. 44g   Diet. Fiber 28g   Prot. 11g

Breakfast Frittata

1 pastry crust
  or biscuit
  or bread dough

Smashed Potatoes
  (recipe below)

Linda's Scrambled Tofu
  (recipe at right)

4 vegetarian breakfast
  links, sliced

SMASHED POTATOES:

6 to 8 Red Bliss
  potatoes

Soy milk (as needed)

Salt to taste

Onion or garlic salt
  (optional)

LINDA'S SCRAMBLED TOFU:

1 pound firm
  water-packed
  tofu, rinsed
  and drained

1 12.3-ounce package
  firm or extra-
  firm Mori-Nu
  Tofu

¼ cup nutritional
  yeast

1½ tablespoons
  chicken-like
  seasoning

2 teaspoons beef-like
  seasoning

1 teaspoon Vege-Sal
  (to taste)

¼ teaspoon garlic
  powder

¼ cup water

1 bunch green onions,
  chopped

Imitation bacon bits

Line springform pan or pie plate with pastry crust or biscuit or bread dough. Cover bottom with Smashed Potatoes (directions below). Add the scrambled tofu (directions below). Arrange sliced vegetarian links on top. Bake at 350 degrees for 15 to 20 minutes, or until layers are heated through.

For variety try using veggie sausage crumbles or other vegetarian meat substitutes. You can make this ahead of time. Bake 20 minutes before serving. Serve hot!
—Brenda

For Smashed Potatoes: Boil potatoes until tender. Mash with soy milk to desired consistency. Add seasonings.

For Linda's Scrambled Tofu: Rinse and drain water-packed tofu. Crumble both kinds of tofu into a mixing bowl. Add seasonings and set aside.

Sauté 1 cup chopped green onion in water until water is gone. Mix in seasoned tofu and simmer for approximately 15 to 20 minutes. Garnish with vegetarian bacon bits.

Yields 8 to 10 servings

Per serving: Cal. 320   Fat 11g   Sat. fat 2.4g   Sod. 685mg   Carb. 42g   Diet. Fiber 4g   Prot. 14.6g

Fruit Soup

Bring half of the pineapple juice to a boil, stir in tapioca, and boil 4 minutes. Remove from heat; add remaining juice. Mix well and add rest of ingredients. Put in refrigerator and chill well before serving.

Serve in bowls with sliced bananas on top.

When I attended Wisconsin Academy, our cook would make Fruit Soup and homemade cinnamon rolls every Friday night for supper. I looked forward to it all week long. I still like Fruit Soup and serve it to my family when they want a light supper. It is also excellent for a brunch or luncheon. —Cinda

1 46-ounce can pineapple juice

½ cup tapioca

1 16-ounce can diced peaches, drained

1 15-ounce can diced pears, drained

3 cups fresh or frozen blueberries

1 15¼-ounce can crushed pineapple

1 6-ounce can frozen grape juice concentrate

Yields 24 ½-cup servings

Per serving: Cal. 94 Fat 0.1g Sat. fat 0.2g Sod. 3.86mg Carb. 24.2g Diet. Fiber 0.8g Prot. 0.4g

Soups, Salads, & Sandwiches

Minestrone Soup
p. 58

Green Pea
Picnic Salad
p. 63

Blackened Tofu Salad
With Strawberry
Dressing
p. 60

Falafel Pita Pockets
p. 67

Autumn Stew

1 medium-size buttercup or butternut squash

1 to 2 tablespoons olive oil

1 ½-pound package baby carrots, sliced

1 medium onion, finely diced

1 28-ounce can diced tomatoes

1½ cups mild salsa

2 15-ounce cans black beans, drained and rinsed

2 teaspoons Vege-Sal, optional

½ cup Tofutti Better Than Sour Cream for garnish

1 small bunch fresh parsley for garnish

Bake squash and cube.

In a large skillet over medium heat, combine olive oil, carrots, and onion. Sauté until tender. Add the tomatoes, salsa, black beans, and Vege-Sal. Simmer approximately 15 minutes. Add the cubed squash and continue simmering another 10 minutes.

Garnish each serving in the middle with one tablespoon Better Than Sour Cream and a piece of parsley.

Serve with hot dinner rolls, a garden salad, and your favorite dessert.
—Linda

Yields 8 1-cup servings

Per serving: Cal. 249 Fat 5g Sat. fat 1.4g Sod. 810mg Carb. 43g Diet. Fiber 8.9g Prot. 10.5g

In a gallon-sized kettle, combine 8 cups water, potatoes, celery, Vege-Sal, and celery salt. Bring to a boil, and then reduce heat to medium.

In a blender combine the ½ cup water with onion; blend until the onion is liquid. Add to the soup; cook until potatoes and celery are tender, about 20 minutes.

In blender, combine tofu, Better Than Cream Cheese, soy milk, and cornstarch. Blend until smooth and add to the soup. Stir and ladle into bowls. Sprinkle parsley, chives, or veggie cheese on top of each serving. Serve with your favorite crackers.

For a more colorful soup, add ½ cup shredded carrot to the soup when it is almost done cooking. This soup is also good made the day before you want to serve it. —Linda

- 8 cups plus ½ cup water
- 10 medium potatoes, diced
- 1 cup diced celery
- 1 tablespoon Vege-Sal
- 1 tablespoon celery salt, optional
- 1 medium onion, chopped
- 1 12.3-ounce package Mori-Nu Silken Tofu
- 4 ounces herb flavor Tofutti Better Than Cream Cheese
- 1 cup soy milk
- 3 tablespoons cornstarch
- ½ cup shredded carrots (optional)
- Parsley, chives, or veggie cheese for garnish

Makes 12 cups

Per serving: Cal. 135   Fat 3.7g   Sat. fat 2.45g   Sod. 433mg   Carb. 21g   Diet. Fiber 2g   Prot. 5g

Southwestern Bean Soup

1 large onion, chopped

1 clove garlic, minced fine

1 teaspoon olive oil

2 quarts canned tomatoes, diced

1 to 2 tablespoons McKay's Chicken Style Seasoning

2 cups water

2 15-ounce cans black beans, rinsed and drained

1 16-ounce can kidney beans, rinsed and drained

1 15-ounce can great northern beans, rinsed and drained

1 15-ounce can pinto beans, rinsed and drained

1 cup corn, raw or frozen

2 teaspoons ground cumin

2 teaspoons chili powder

¼ teaspoon hot pepper sauce

In a large cooking pot, sauté onion and garlic in olive oil until tender. Stir in the remaining ingredients; bring to a boil. Reduce heat and simmer, uncovered, for 30 minutes. Serve hot!

I love this soup on a cold day, but it tastes so good you don't have to wait for winter to enjoy it! Try adding a variety of different beans just for something different. If you like your soup a little spicier, add a tablespoon of jalapeño peppers. Now that will warm you up! —Brenda

Serves 10 to 12

Per serving: Cal. 222 Fat 1.5g Sat. fat 0.2g Sod. 610mg Carb. 41.7g Diet. Fiber 11.9g Prot. 12.3g

White Chili

In a large saucepan, combine all ingredients and bring to a boil. Reduce heat and simmer, uncovered, for 30 minutes. Serve hot.

Try serving this chili in bread bowls with Tofutti Sour Supreme and a sprinkle of fresh or dried chopped chives for garnish. Add a fresh salad to complete your menu. —Cinda

1 medium onion, chopped and sautéed

2 cups water

2 tablespoons McKay's Chicken Style Seasoning

1 tablespoon chopped garlic

1 4-ounce can chopped green chiles

1 teaspoon salt, optional

½ teaspoon cumin

1 teaspoon dried oregano

1½ teaspoons cayenne

1 12-ounce container Tofutti Sour Supreme

2 15.5-ounce cans great northern beans, rinsed and drained

2 12.5-ounce cans Worthington FriChik, including juice

Serves 8 to 10

Per serving: Cal. 153 Fat 7.4g Sat. fat 2.7g Sod. 465mg Carb. 13g Diet. Fiber 2.5g Prot. 9.6g

Minestrone Soup

2 quarts canned
   tomatoes

1 quart water

2 large onions, diced

3 stalks celery, diced

¼ cup uncooked
   barley

3 raw carrots, diced

1 cup raw okra

2 cups chopped raw
   cabbage

2 cups raw green
   beans, cut into
   bite-size pieces

2 cups diced raw
   zucchini

1 large potato, cut
   into bite-size
   pieces

1 16-ounce can pinto
   beans

1 16-ounce can white
   northern beans

1 16-ounce can black
   beans

1 to 2 tablespoons
   Italian seasoning

Garlic salt or powder
   to taste

6 to 8 imitation
   chicken bouillon
   cubes

½ cup mini shells or
   other small pasta
   (optional)

In large soup pan, combine tomatoes, water, onions, celery, and barley. Bring to a boil and slow boil until barley is tender. Add remaining ingredients (except pasta) and add water as needed. Simmer approximately 1 to 2 hours until vegetables are tender.

If adding pasta, add 15 minutes before cooking is complete. Enjoy!

If you love vegetables, you are going to love this soup. Don't be afraid to add or take away vegetables. I usually use whatever I have on hand at the time, so my soup comes out different every meal! You might notice that I did not list any salt. That is because there is salt in the bouillon cubes. You can substitute shell pasta for any small pasta. —Brenda

Yields 12 to 14 cups

Per serving: Cal. 158   Fat 0.8g   Sat. fat 0.1g   Sod. 261mg   Carb. 31.7g   Diet. Fiber 9.3g   Prot. 8.2g

Garden Tabbouleh Salad

In a medium bowl, combine bulgur and salt and boiling water. Cover and let soak 20 minutes until tender; drain if necessary.

From lemon, grate two teaspoons zest and squeeze three tablespoons juice and add to bulgur. Add rest of ingredients and toss gently to mix.

Serving ideas: Spoon over a bed of lettuce or in a hollowed-out tomato as a salad; spoon into hollowed-out cherry tomatoes as a healthy appetizer; or use as a sandwich filling in pita bread.

This salad reminds me of my dad's garden. When I was a child, my brothers and sisters and I were all expected to help care for the garden. I loved to walk barefoot in the soft dirt and eat cucumbers and tomatoes fresh from the vine! —Cinda

1 cup bulgur wheat

1 teaspoon salt

2 cups boiling water

1 lemon

1 red bell pepper, chopped

1 16-ounce can chickpeas, rinsed

1 pint grape tomatoes, cut in half

¼ cup chopped raw basil or parsley

3 tablespoons extra virgin olive oil

2 cups chopped pickling cucumber or European cucumber

Salt to taste

Serves 8 to 10

Per serving: Cal. 152 Fat 5g Sat. fat 0.7g Sod. 289mg Carb. 24g Diet. Fiber 5.7g Prot. 4.6g

Blackened Tofu Salad
With Strawberry Dressing

1 cup whole pecans

1 package water-packed
   extra-firm tofu

Tofu breading
   (recipe below)

1 tablespoon olive oil

2 16-ounce packages
   mixed salad greens

2 cups sliced raw
   strawberries
   plus two whole

1 5-ounce can mandarin
   orange sections,
   reserving 5 or 6
   sections

Strawberry dressing
   (recipe at right)

TOFU BREADING:

½ cup of unbleached
   white flour

1½ teaspoons McKay's
   Beef Style
   Seasoning

1½ teaspoons McKay's
   Chicken Style
   Seasoning

1½ teaspoons Vege-Sal,
   optional

¼ teaspoon onion powder

½ teaspoon paprika

¼ teaspoon basil

⅛ teaspoon cayenne
   (to taste)

STRAWBERRY
DRESSING:

½ cup frozen
   strawberries

1 package Mori-Nu
   Silken Tofu

½ cup cold water

¼ cup soy milk
   powder

3 tablespoons pure
   maple syrup

1 whole strawberry

Place pecans on a glass plate. Microwave on high for 4 to 5 minutes, until toasted. (Pecans will be fragrant when toasted.) Set aside. (Pecans firm as they cool.)

Rinse tofu well. On a plate covered with a paper towel, place tofu. Cover with plastic wrap. Set a 5-pound container on top of the tofu for 15 to 20 minutes to squeeze out the water. Slice tofu into eight slices. Dip in olive oil and then in breading. In a very hot skillet, fry until slightly blackened. Remove from skillet and set aside. When cool cut into strips.

In a glass bowl, layer the salad ingredients: ⅓ of the mixed greens, ⅓ of the strawberry slices, ⅓ of the pecans, ⅓ of the mixed greens, orange sections, the remaining pecans, lettuce, and strawberry slices. Top with tofu. Place whole strawberry in the middle of the salad; mandarin orange sections around the strawberry. Serve with strawberry dressing (directions below).

For strawberry dressing: Partially thaw strawberries by microwaving on high for about 1 minute. In blender combine all ingredients. Blend until smooth. Garnish with whole strawberry.

For variety and color, add a cup of raw blueberries to the salad. This salad is great for that extra special occasion. —Linda

Serves 4 to 5

Salad with dressing: Cal. 464   Fat 25g   Sat. fat 6g   Sod. 479mg   Carb. 47g   Diet. Fiber 6.1g   Prot. 20.4g

Southwestern Couscous Salad

Put two teaspoons olive oil in a medium frying pan. Over medium heat, sauté onion with garlic until onion is translucent.

In a large salad bowl, combine all ingredients except water, couscous, and salt.

In a small saucepan, bring water to a boil. Add couscous and salt. Remove from heat and cover. Leave covered for 5 minutes. Combine with other ingredients in salad bowl. May serve warm as a side dish or chill for 2 to 3 hours and serve over a bed of lettuce for a salad.

My inspiration for this dish came from my dad. He has a wonderful way of mixing a variety of unique foods in various ways and always came up with a new and delicious creation! —Cinda

1 medium onion, chopped fine

2 teaspoons minced garlic

2 teaspoons plus 2 tablespoons olive oil

1 15-ounce can black beans, drained and rinsed

2 cups frozen sweet corn, thawed

3 tablespoons apple cider vinegar

1 tablespoon lime juice

1 teaspoon Sucanat Granulated Cane Juice

2 teaspoons chili powder

½ teaspoon cumin

¼ teaspoon cayenne

1 cup chopped carrots

1 cup chopped celery

¼ cup chopped pickled jalapeño peppers

1 cup water

1 cup couscous

1 teaspoon salt

Serves 8 to 10

Per serving: Cal. 224 Fat 3.8g Sat. fat 0.5g Sod. 509mg Carb. 42.7g Diet. Fiber 6.1g Prot. 8.2g

Potato Salad

6 cups cooked diced potatoes

⅓ cup diced dill pickles

¼ cup sliced green olives

1 cup of Vegenaise

1 scant teaspoon Vege-Sal, optional

1½ teaspoons onion powder

Radish roses, parsley, carrots, or imitation bacon bits for garnish

Place cooked, diced potatoes in a large bowl. Add pickles and green olives.

In another bowl, combine Vegenaise. Stir remaining ingredients into the Vegenaise. Stir the seasoned Vegenaise into the potato mixture. Chill for about 4 hours before serving.

After chilling, taste to see if the salad needs more seasoning.

This salad is best if made the day before you want to serve it to give the seasonings time to blend together. I sometimes add 1 to 2 cups of black olives to this recipe. Celery, carrots, and radishes can also be added. However, I have found that the simpler the foods are prepared, the easier it is to please large groups of people. —Linda

Serves 5 to 6

Per serving: Cal. 409 Fat 27.1g Sat. fat 4g Sod. 758mg Carb. 39g Diet. Fiber 5.5g

Green Pea Picnic Salad

Mix all ingredients together in large bowl. Stir well to coat all vegetables. May serve at once, or chill up to 24 hours.

For variety I sometimes add cooked pasta, such as penne or mini shells, to this recipe. I have also served it on a bed of Romaine lettuce or field greens as a main course for a luncheon or brunch. —**Cinda**

1 pound frozen petite green peas, thawed but not cooked

1 cup chopped cucumber

1 clove raw garlic, minced

¼ cup chopped fresh dill

1 red bell pepper, chopped

1 onion, chopped and sautéed until translucent

⅔ cup Tofutti Better Than Sour Cream

⅓ cup Grapeseed Oil Vegenaise

2 tablespoons lemon juice

Salt to taste

Serves 8 to 10

Per serving: Cal. 121   Fat 7.7g   Sat. fat 1.9g   Sod. 149mg   Carb. 10.3g   Diet. Fiber 3.1g   Prot. 3.4g

Cranberry Fruit Salad

1 6-ounce can cranberry sauce

1 6-ounce can crushed pineapple, drained

2 cups nondairy whipped topping plus more for garnish

1 cup chopped pecans

Mix all ingredients and pour into a gelatin mold or an 8 x 8-inch glass pan. Freeze for approximately 8 hours. Remove from mold and place on plate. Cut into 9 squares. Garnish with raw cranberries and leaf lettuce. You can add a dollop of nondairy whipped topping on the very top.

I like to keep this dish in the freezer so that it is always handy for unexpected company because it is so easy to make! There are only four ingredients! You can use other nuts, but pecans are my favorite! —Brenda

Yields 9 servings

Per serving: Cal. 168 Fat 8g Sat. fat 6.5g Sod. 21mg Carb. 23g Diet. Fiber 1g Prot. 1g

Vege-Tofu Burgers

2 large onions

2 packages tofu, any kind

3 tablespoons Better Than Milk soy milk (more as needed)

5 to 6 cups seasoned bread crumbs

4 to 5 cups quick oats

2 cups crushed saltine crackers

2 cups chopped pecans

2 packets Good Seasons Italian Dressing Mix

2 cups cooked lentils

1 cup cooked rice (white or brown)

In a blender or food processor, blend together tofu, onions, and 3 tablespoons soy milk.

Mix all ingredients together. Shape into balls slightly larger than a golf ball, adding a little more soy milk if necessary.

On a cookie sheet sprayed with a nonstick cooking spray, place balls and flatten into burgers. Bake for 30 minutes at 375 degrees until golden, flipping burgers after the first 15 minutes. Serve hot on a wheat bun.

Optional: Burgers may be fried in olive or grape seed oil instead of baking.

These vege-burgers can be made ahead of time and kept in the freezer. In fact, I almost always have them in my freezer! Sometimes I put them in a 9 x 13-inch pan, cover them with tomato soup or a nondairy mushroom soup and bake for one hour at 350 degrees for a main dish. Add a vegetable, green salad, and some homemade wheat bread, and you have a dinner special enough to serve guests! —Brenda

Yields 24 burgers

Per burger: Cal. 288 Fat 9g Sat. fat 2.7g Sod. 948mg Carb. 42g Diet. Fiber 5g Prot. 11g

Potato-Spinach Burrito

In a skillet over medium heat, heat olive oil and sauté onions and garlic. When onions are translucent, add potatoes, spinach, tomatoes, and salt. Set this filling aside.

In a medium skillet over medium heat, heat beans. On each flour tortilla, spread a small amount of refried beans and add a small amount of filling. Roll the tortilla and serve. Garnish with guacamole if desired.
—Brenda

1 tablespoon olive oil

2 medium onions, diced

1 to 2 garlic cloves, finely minced

3 cups diced cooked potatoes

4 to 6 cups raw spinach

2 cups diced tomatoes

Salt to taste

1 to 2 cups refried beans

6 flour tortillas

Guacamole (optional)
Recipe on p. 22

Yields 6 burritos

Per burrito: Cal. 436   Fat 11.6g   Sat. fat 3.1g   Sod. 466mg   Carb. 71.5g   Diet. Fiber 9.1g   Prot. 13g

Potato Corn Chowder

In a large cooking pot, combine potatoes, onions, salt, and enough water to cover potatoes. Bring to a boil. Turn heat down and cook, covered, until potatoes are tender. The water should be almost gone. (You may add additional water as needed to cook potatoes.) When potatoes are tender, add corn, celery salt, and enough soy milk to reach a soup consistency.

If you like a thicker soup, mix together cornstarch and water and add to the simmering soup until desired thickness is obtained. Cook for an additional 15 minutes after adding cornstarch. Do not bring to a boil after adding soy milk because doing so will change the consistency. Serve hot! —Brenda

3 medium potatoes, peeled and diced

1 medium onion, finely diced

1 teaspoon salt

2 cans cream-style corn

½ teaspoon celery salt

1 to 2 cups plain soy milk

Yields 6 cups

Per serving: Cal. 172   Fat 1.46g   Sat. fat 0.2g   Sod. 799mg   Carb. 39.5g   Diet. Fiber 3.5g   Prot. 5g

Barbecue Vege-Beef

1 medium onion, diced fine

½ cup plus 1½ cups water

1 10¾-ounce can reduced sodium tomato soup

1 cup fruit-sweetened catsup

1 tablespoon Bragg Liquid Aminos

1 teaspoon Vege-Sal, optional

1 teaspoon Sucanat Granulated Cane Juice

1 1-pound, 4-ounce can Worthington Vegetarian Burger

¼ cup vegetarian bacon bits, optional

Homemade buns

In a large skillet over medium heat, sauté onion in water until translucent. Stir in tomato soup, catsup, Bragg Liquid Aminos, water, Vege-Sal, sugar, vegetarian burger, and bacon bits. Let simmer 15 to 20 minutes on low. Serve hot with your favorite homemade buns.

Barbecue Vege-Beef is also good served cold in a sandwich the next day.
—Linda

Serves 5 to 6

Per serving: Cal. 289 Fat 6.6g Sat. fat 0.6g Sod. 1040mg Carb. 40g Diet. Fiber 4g Prot. 20g

Falafel Pita Pockets

Preheat oven to 400 degrees.

Rinse and drain chickpeas. Combine all ingredients in a food processor and process until smooth. (If you do not have a food processor, you can use a potato masher.)

Spray a baking sheet with a nonstick cooking spray. Form mixture into patties approximately 3 inches in diameter. Place on baking sheet*. Spray each patty with the nonstick cooking spray. Bake for 20 to 25 minutes until golden brown. Flip over halfway through cooking time. Serve warm or cold in pita bread with cucumber sauce (directions below).

* Falafel can also be pan fried in 1 to 2 tablespoons olive oil.

These are great for picnics or sack lunches, but pack the ingredients separately and assemble the sandwiches just before eating. Otherwise the pocket bread can get soggy. —**Cinda**

For cucumber sauce: Wash cucumbers, peel (if desired), and dice. Wash, seed, and dice tomato. Combine all ingredients in a medium-size bowl. Mix well. Add soy milk if sauce is too thick.

This sauce is also delicious with other sandwiches and your favorite Indian food.

¼ cup diced onion

2 cups cooked chickpeas

1 clove fresh garlic, minced

1 teaspoon cumin

½ teaspoon turmeric

½ teaspoon salt

¼ cup fresh parsley or dried equivalent

1/3 cup water

2 teaspoons fresh lemon juice

1 cup cooked bulgur wheat

¼ cup flour

Dash of cayenne

Pita bread

Cucumber sauce (recipe below)

CUCUMBER SAUCE:

2 small cucumbers (pickling or miniature English)

1 small tomato

1½ cups Tofutti Better Than Sour Cream

2 teaspoons Vege-sal (or your favorite seasoned salt)

Dash cayenne pepper

Soy milk (as needed)

Serves 6

Sandwich total: Cal. 347 Fat 12g Sat. fat 4g Sod. 879mg Carb. 51.6g Diet. Fiber 7.6g Prot. 12g
Sauce: Cal. 117 Fat 10g Sat. fat 4g Sod. 302mg Carb. 4.5g Diet. Fiber 6g Prot. 2.5g

Sloppy Joes

1 to 2 cups Soy Add-Ums or 1 12-ounce package Yves Veggie Ground Round (or vegetarian burger of your choice)

1 medium onion, diced

¼ cup diced celery

1 tablespoon olive oil

¾ cup catsup

½ cup water

3 tablespoons lemon juice

1 tablespoon Florida Crystals Milled Cane Sugar

1 tablespoon vegetarian Worcestershire sauce

2 tablespoons apple cider vinegar

1 tablespoon prepared mustard

8 to 12 hamburger buns

Rehydrate Soy Add-Ums according to package instructions. Drain in a strainer and squeeze out excess water. Set aside.

In a large skillet over medium heat, sauté onion and celery in olive oil until tender. Add remaining ingredients except for Soy Add-Ums. Simmer sauce for 15 minutes and then add the Soy Add-Ums. Simmer for 30 minutes. Serve hot over buns.

If you like a "sloppier" sandwich, double the sauce ingredients of this recipe.
—Brenda

Yields 8 to 12 servings

Per serving: Cal. 165 Fat 3.7g Sat. fat 0.5g Sod. 403mg Carb. 30g Diet. Fiber 4.7g Prot. 6.8g

Mock Turkey Subs

In a medium bowl, mix together flour, beef- and chicken-style seasonings, Vege-Sal, onion and garlic powders, and yeast flakes to make a breading mix. Slice tofu into 12 ½-inch slices and dip in breading mix.

In a nonstick skillet over medium heat, heat olive oil and fry tofu until golden brown and slightly crisp. Turn over and fry the other side. Place a half slice of tofu cheese on each piece of tofu and remove skillet from heat. (The cheese will melt only slightly.) Spread each sub bun with Vegenaise and place three half slices of tofu on each sub. Layer the rest of the ingredients in any order.

Tofu can also be cooked in the oven on a cookie sheet with olive or canola oil. This sandwich is good served with a little Italian dressing on the top.
—Linda

½ cup unbleached white flour

1½ teaspoons McKay's Beef Style Seasoning

1½ teaspoons McKay's Chicken Style Seasoning

1½ teaspoons Vege-Sal, optional

¼ teaspoon onion powder

⅛ teaspoon garlic powder

¼ cup nutritional yeast

1 pound water-packed tofu, rinsed and drained

4 slices Tofutti Soy Cheese Slices, cut in half, optional

2 tablespoons olive oil

4 6-inch sub buns

Vegenaise to taste

1 head green leaf lettuce

4 medium-size tomatoes

1 cup sliced olives

2 cucumbers

Lemon pickles to taste

2 yellow peppers

1 sweet red onion

Yields 4 6-inch sandwiches

Per serving: Cal. 463 Fat 19.3g Sat. fat 2g Sod. 856mg Carb. 55.6g Diet. Fiber 3g Prot. 18g

Entrees & Side Dishes

Vegetable
Pot Pie
p. 85

Holiday
Meatless Loaf
p. 76

Mashed
Potatoes
p. 81

Stuffed Squash
p. 82

Old Fashioned Beef Stew

VEGGIE STYLE

Double pie crust recipe of your choice

6 cups water

8 imitation beef bouillon cubes

2 teaspoons Kitchen Bouquet or any vegetarian browning sauce

1 medium onion, diced

2 celery stalks, cut in ½-inch slices

1 cup sliced raw carrots

2 cups Dressler's Soy Add-Ums or a chunky wheat gluten product of your choice

4 medium potatoes, cut into four to six pieces each

¼ cup cold water

4 tablespoons cornstarch

Divide pie dough in half and roll out. Line bottom and sides of a 9 x 13-inch casserole dish with one half. Set aside.

In a large stockpot, combine water, bouillon cubes, and Kitchen Bouquet. Bring to a boil and add onion, celery, carrots, and the Soy Add-Ums or wheat gluten product that is in ¾-inch to 1-inch chunks. When carrots are almost tender, add potatoes. (Potato chunks should be fairly large.)

When potatoes are tender, in a measuring cup mix cornstarch into ¼ cup cold water, stirring until smooth. Stirring constantly, add cornstarch mixture to stew. If desired thickness has been reached, do not add all the cornstarch mixture. Pour stew mixture into the lined casserole dish. Roll out remaining dough and cut air vents. *(I like to draw pictures of a flower or some sort of design on top just to make it look pretty!)* Place pie crust dough on top of the casserole dish and flute or pinch together top and bottom crust edges. Bake immediately at 350 degrees for approximately 1 hour until crust is golden and flaky.

This is just like the old fashioned beef stew that "Grandma used to make." I also like to prepare it with biscuits instead of pie crust: Prepare biscuit recipe of your choice. Pour the stew into a 9 x 13-inch pan and then place unbaked biscuits on top till the entire stew is covered with biscuits. Bake at 400 degrees for 13 to 15 minutes, until biscuits are golden.

If you don't like biscuits or pie crust, the stew is ready after you have thickened it on the stove. You can serve it just like that. Serve some good homemade wheat bread with it and enjoy! —**Brenda**

Serves 12 to 14

Per serving: Cal. 251 Fat 13g Sat. fat .9g Sod. 706mg Carb. 29g Diet. Fiber 2.6g Prot. 5g

Lasagna Roll-Ups

Blend cashews and water together until smooth and creamy. Add Better Than Cream Cheese, garlic powder, Vege-Sal, onion powder, and lemon juice, and blend until smooth.

In a mixing bowl, crumble tofu. Add dried parsley. Fold cashew mixture into the tofu mixture. Add spinach, if desired.

Cook lasagna noodles according to package directions. Rinse with cold water. Cut each noodle in half, width-wise. Place a heaping tablespoon filling onto the noodle half and fold over a couple of times, as you would an enchilada.

Spray a 9 x 13-inch baking dish with nonstick cooking spray. Pour all but 1/2 cup spaghetti sauce on the bottom of the baking dish and sprinkle with garlic powder. Place lasagna roll-ups on top of the sauce, seam side down. Spoon remaining spaghetti sauce down the middle of each lasagna roll-up; leaving ends of roll-ups showing. Cover with foil and bake at 350 degrees for about 30 minutes, or until hot and bubbly.

Garnish with parsley or parmesan.

This recipe can be made ahead and frozen or served right away. The texture does change somewhat when frozen, but it is still good. —Linda

1 cup chopped cashews

1 cup cold water

1 8-ounce container herb flavor Tofutti Better Than Cream Cheese

1 teaspoon garlic powder (to taste)

1 teaspoon Vege-Sal

1 teaspoon onion powder

1 tablespoon lemon juice

2 12.3-ounce packages Mori-Nu Tofu

2 teaspoons dried parsley flakes

1 cup frozen chopped spinach, thawed and squeezed dry (optional)

1 16-ounce package lasagna noodles

1 26-ounce can or 1 1-pound, 10.5-ounce jar spaghetti sauce

Garlic powder to taste

Fresh parsley or vegan parmesan for garnish

Serves 6 to 8

Per roll-up: Cal. 502   Fat 21.7g   Sat. fat 9.5g   Sod. 874mg   Carb. 60.4g   Diet. Fiber 5.7g   Prot. 19.2g

Holiday Meatless Loaf

1 onion, chopped

¼ cup soy milk plus
more to moisten

1 12.3-ounce package
soft tofu

1 12-ounce package
Yves Veggie
Ground Round

3 cups quick oats

1 to 2 cups finely
chopped pecans

3 cups stuffing mix or
seasoned bread
crumbs

2 packages Good
Seasons Italian
Dressing Mix

1 cup catsup

1 10¾-ounce can
reduced sodium
tomato soup

1 can water

Combine onion, ¼ cup soy milk, and tofu in food processor and mix until smooth. Add veggie ground round, oats, pecans, stuffing mix, and Italian dressing mix. Moisten with soy milk until all ingredients stick together. Pour into a 9 x 13-inch baking dish and shape into loaf, leaving at least two inches of space on each side of loaf. Bake at 375 degrees for 30 minutes.

Remove from oven and cover top of loaf with catsup.

Combine tomato soup and water. Pour around sides of loaf in pan. Return to oven and bake at 375 degrees for 30 to 40 minutes. Serve hot.

I created this recipe especially for my husband, Tim, who recently became a vegetarian. He has always loved hamburger meatloaf. He does not like the texture of many vegetarian meat substitutes, so I worked hard to come up with a meatloaf substitute. He loves this recipe so much that he told me he doesn't even miss the hamburger! Leftovers make wonderful sandwiches.
—Brenda

Yields 10 to 12 ½-cup servings

Per serving: Cal. 327   Fat 13.3g   Sat. fat 1.8g   Sod. 1060mg   Carb. 41.3g   Diet. Fiber 4.7g   Prot. 12.8g

Veggie Chicken & Dressing

In a large skillet over medium heat, sauté onion and celery in the two teaspoons margarine.

Make broth of hot water, McKay's Chicken-Style Seasoning, and the 1 tablespoon margarine.

In a large bowl, crumble Fri-Chik and combine all ingredients. Place in a greased 9 x 13-inch casserole dish. Bake at 350 degrees for 1 hour.

For special occasions you can wrap mixture in puff pastry and bake!

My mom has the wonderful ability to take any recipe and serve it in many different ways. Her creativity is an inspiration to me. I have made this recipe and wrapped puff pastry all around it. I then decorate it with leaves or flowers cut out of pastry and bake it on a large cookie sheet. It is an elegant dish you can be proud to serve to anyone. And the best part? It's delicious!
—Cinda

1 large onion, chopped

1 cup chopped celery

1 tablespoon plus 2 teaspoons margarine

1 cup hot water

1 tablespoon McKay's Chicken Style Seasoning

4 12.5-ounce cans Worthington FriChik, drained

1 cup soy milk

6 cups stuffing mix

1 12.3-ounce package Mori-Nu Soft Tofu

Thyme to taste

Sage to taste

Serves 10 to 12

Per serving: Cal. 291 Fat 11.4g Sat. fat 3.9g Sod. 997mg Carb. 31.7g Diet. Fiber 1.5g Prot. 17.2g

Sweet & Sour Meatballs

VEGGIE STYLE

1 12.3-ounce package
Mori-Nu Tofu

1 medium onion

1 teaspoon Vege-Sal
(or your favorite
seasoned salt),
optional

¼ teaspoon garlic
powder

1 tablespoon Bragg
Liquid Aminos
or soy sauce

1 cup pecan meal

1½ cups finely
crushed saltine
crackers or bread
crumbs

Sweet & sour sauce
(recipe below)

SWEET & SOUR
SAUCE:

1 8-ounce can tomato
sauce

1 cup apricot Simply
100 Percent Fruit

½ teaspoon Vege–Sal,
optional

¼ teaspoon cumin

Dash salt

Juice from 1 lemon

In a blender, blend tofu, onion, Vege-Sal, garlic powder, and liquid aminos till smooth. Place blended mixture into a mixing bowl and stir in pecan meal and crackers. When completely mixed together, form into balls.

Spray two cookie sheets with a nonstick cooking spray. Place meatballs on sheets. Bake at 350 degrees 30 to 45 minutes, until golden brown.

Put baked meatballs in baking dish, cover with sweet and sour sauce (directions below), and return to oven. Bake until bubbly.

Garnish with fresh parsley.

For sweet & sour sauce: Mix all ingredients together. Cook over medium-high heat until hot and bubbling.

This recipe is great to make ahead and freeze. For variety, try different sauces. For a crunchy ball, add ½ cup of chopped pecans to the recipe. I also have used this recipe to make a loaf or patties. —Linda

Serves 4 to 5

Per serving: Cal. 488 Fat 4g Sat. fat 4.5g Sod. 785mg Carb. 94g Diet. Fiber 2.6g Prot. 25g

Tatyana's Meatballs

VEGGIE STYLE

In a frying pan over medium heat, sauté diced onion in olive oil until translucent and tender. Pour into a large mixing bowl, adding all other ingredients except soy milk and bread crumbs. Mix well, adding enough soy milk to moisten until dough just holds together. (If mixture gets too wet, add dry bread crumbs or oats.) Shape into 1-inch balls and roll in the dry bread crumbs. Sauté breaded balls in olive oil until browned. Drain on paper towels to absorb excess oil.

This recipe was inspired by my first trip to Russia. Tatyana, the conference president's wife, made a dish similar to this one. I loved it so much that I came home and tried to re-create it. Of course many of the ingredients in Russia were not available here, so I had to improvise a lot! Amazingly, they are very similar and absolutely delicious! These balls can be made ahead of time and frozen. —**Brenda**

1 medium onion, finely diced

2 teaspoons plus 2 tablespoons olive oil

1 teaspoon garlic powder

2½ cups chopped walnuts

1 cup shredded soy cheese

2 tablespoons parsley

3 cups oats

1 teaspoon salt

Soy milk, as needed to moisten

2 cups dry bread crumbs or finely crushed Rusks (recipe on p. 127)

Serves 8 to 10

Per serving: Cal. 431 Fat 26g Sat. fat 2.6g Sod. 931mg Carb. 40g Diet. Fiber 5.5g Prot. 13.6g

Cinda's Homemade Gluten

1 to 2 teaspoons
Vege-Sal, optional

3 cups quick gluten
flour

½ cup whole-wheat
flour

3 cups plus 12 cups
warm water

¼ cup plus ½ cup
Bragg Liquid
Aminos

3 tablespoons olive oil

3 tablespoons Vegex

1 large onion, chopped

2 cups chopped celery

2 cloves of garlic,
minced

In a large bowl, mix Vege-Sal and flours. Combine 3 cups water with ¼ cup liquid aminos. Add water mixture to flour mixture and knead with hands quickly and thoroughly. Form this gluten mixture into long roll, about 2½ inches in diameter. Slice into pieces about ½-inch thick. Pat gluten pieces into circles.

In a large stockpot combine 12 cups water, olive oil, 3 tablespoons Vegex, ½ cup liquid aminos, onion, celery, and garlic. Bring to a boil. Add sliced gluten and boil gently for about 30 minutes. Lower heat and continue cooking for another 30 minutes. Let cool, and then store in containers with a little of the broth. Can or freeze.

Never mix more than two batches of dough at a time because you have to mix the ingredients together quickly and this is very difficult to do in large quantities. *(Through trial and error I have learned that the gluten has a better texture when I make it in small batches.)*

I like to dip the gluten in flour or bread crumbs and bake on a cookie sheet that has been sprayed with nonstick cooking spray, spraying the top of the gluten also. I bake it at 350 degrees for 20 to 25 minutes, turning once. The gluten can be served with a mushroom sauce and is a wonderful addition to soups, stews, and oriental dishes.

I like this recipe because it does not require all the rinsing that usual gluten recipes require. It is easy to make and also very versatile. You can make it into any shape you want depending on the recipe requirements. You can bake it, fry it, or barbecue it! —**Cinda**

Serves 8 to 10

Per serving: Cal. 365   Fat 4g   Sat. fat 0.6g   Sod. 1040mg   Carb. 51.5g   Diet. Fiber 1.4g   Prot. 27g

Mashed Potatoes

Peel potatoes, place in a 1-gallon kettle, and cover with hot water. Bring to a boil. Cook over medium-high heat for 20 minutes or until tender. Drain, saving about 4 cups of the potato water.

In a large bowl place hot potatoes, Vege-Sal, Better Than Cream Cheese, and soy margarine. Whip together, adding potato water to achieve desired consistency. Serve with brown gravy (directions below).

You can also use red potatoes and mash with the skins on.

For brown gravy: In a gallon-size kettle, mix together 6 cups water, beef-style seasoning, salt, and liquid aminos. In a blender, purée onion in 2 cups of the water. Add onion purée to other seasoned water.

In a skillet over medium heat, brown flour, stirring constantly. Set aside to cool. Sift out the lumps.

In a separate bowl, mix the browned flour with oil and 2 cups of the seasoned water to make a thin paste. Whip paste into seasoned water and heat on medium high stirring until thick.

I can still feel the delight of coming to the table as a child and seeing a big dish of mashed potatoes and gravy. Such a simple dish, but it put smiles on all our faces. God is so good to us! He gives us so many simple things to enjoy! For simpler mashed potatoes, omit the cream cheese and add ½ teaspoon Vege-Sal. Extra gravy can be used in your favorite vegetable pot pie recipe. —Linda

10 medium baking potatoes

Hot water

Salt to taste

1 teaspoon Vege-Sal, optional

1 8-ounce container herb flavor Tofutti Better Than Cream Cheese

3 tablespoons soy margarine

Brown gravy (recipe below)

BROWN GRAVY:

8 cups cool water

1 tablespoon McKay's Beef Style Seasoning

½ teaspoon salt, optional

½ cup of Bragg Liquid Aminos or soy sauce

1 small onion, blended

1½ cups unbleached white flour

½ cup canola oil

Serves 6 to 8; gravy recipe serves 15

Per serving (potatoes): Cal. 211 Fat 10.2g Sat. fat 2.3g Sod. 195mg Carb. 26.5g Diet. Fiber 2.3g Prot. 4g
Per serving (gravy): Cal. 122 Fat 7.6g Sat. fat 0.6g Sodium 634mg Carb. 10.8g Diet. Fiber 0.5g Prot. 1.0g

Stuffed Squash

1 large Hubbard
    squash
    (or 3 acorn
    or 2 butternut
    squash)

5 cups cooked brown
    rice

3 6-ounce boxes wild
    rice pilaf

1 to 2 onions, finely
    chopped

2 tablespoons
    margarine

2 cups toasted
    almonds

Salt to taste

Garlic powder to taste

Cut top off squash at a 45 degree angle (see suggestion below) and remove seeds. Replace top and bake at 350 degrees for approximately 3 hours, until tender.

Meanwhile, cook wild rice pilaf according to package directions, omitting margarine (may be cooked ahead of time).

In a large skillet over medium heat, sauté onions in margarine until translucent. Add toasted almonds, brown rice, rice pilaf, and seasonings.

When squash is tender, remove from oven and place on serving platter. Fill squash with rice filling and serve hot.

This is a recipe that I like to use for special occasions. It is also one of my favorite recipes to demonstrate at cooking schools because it gets so many oohs and ahhs. Hubbard squash is thick and tough and always hard to cut, so I go to my local grocery store and have someone in the produce department cut it for me. Make sure they cut it at a slant (about 45 degrees) and not straight across. Keep the top portion that they cut off, because you will need it for baking. —**Brenda**

Serves 10 to 12

Per serving: Cal. 529 Fat 15g Sat. fat 2g Sod. 493mg Carb. 89g Diet. Fiber 6g Prot. 14g

Eggplant Casserole

Peel eggplant and slice into ⅛-inch slices. Put eggplant slices in cold water and add salt. Let sit for approximately 10 minutes.

Meanwhile, in a skillet over medium heat, sauté onions in 1 tablespoon olive oil until tender; set aside.

Dip eggplant slices one at a time into seasoned flour (directions below). In a 10 x 15-inch baking pan, evenly distribute two tablespoons olive oil. Place eggplant slices in the pan as closely together as possible—they shrink while baking. Bake at 350 degrees for about 20 to 30 minutes, or until lightly browned on one side. (You do not need to bake them on both sides.)

In a 3-quart baking dish, pour ¼ the jar of spaghetti sauce. Sprinkle garlic powder on top of sauce. Place eggplant, browned side up, on top of the sauce. Put a layer of onions on top of the eggplant, a thin layer of sauce, more garlic powder. Keep layering your pan with sauce, garlic powder, eggplant, onions. End with eggplant. Place in the oven and bake at 350 degrees 20 to 30 minutes, until hot and bubbly.

Garnish with fresh parsley and serve with a vegetable salad, angel hair pasta covered with your favorite sauce, and garlic bread.

This dish is really good with fresh mushrooms sautéed with the onions. It also is good layered with shredded veggie mozzarella cheese.

For seasoned flour: Mix ingredients together in a mixing bowl.

When I make up the seasoned flour mixture, I always make a double batch and put the extra in an airtight container to use for other recipes. I use it to bread my gluten steaks, zucchini, or anything else I bread. —Linda

Ingredients

- 2 large eggplants
- 1 teaspoon salt
- 2 large onions, thinly sliced
- 1 tablespoon plus 2 tablespoons olive oil
- Seasoned flour (recipe below)
- 1 10-ounce jar of spaghetti sauce
- Garlic powder to taste

SEASONED FLOUR:

- 2 cups unbleached white flour
- 1 cup nutritional yeast
- 2 tablespoons McKay's Beef Style Seasoning
- 2 tablespoons McKay's Chicken Style Seasoning
- 2 tablespoons Vege-Sal, optional
- 1 teaspoon onion powder
- ½ teaspoon garlic powder

Serves 6 to 8

Per serving: Cal. 133   Fat 6g   Sat. fat 0.8g   Sod. 662mg   Carb. 16.6g   Diet. Fiber 2g   Prot. 3.7g

Tumbuka Stew Over Putu*

1 large onion, diced

2 tablespoons olive oil

3 small zucchini, sliced

3 small yellow squash, sliced

1 yellow bell pepper, diced into large pieces

1 red bell pepper, diced into large pieces

2 cloves garlic, minced

2 cups chopped portabella mushrooms

1 28-ounce can diced stewed tomatoes

1 14½-ounce can Mexican-style diced tomatoes

1 teaspoon dried rosemary

1 teaspoon dried basil

Salt to taste plus 1 teaspoon

2 cups water

¾ cup polenta**

**Polenta is coarsely ground cornmeal*

In a large skillet, over medium heat, sauté onion in 1 tablespoon of the olive oil until onion is clear. Add the other tablespoon of oil and the rest of the fresh vegetables. Continue cooking until tender. Add canned tomatoes and seasonings. Continue cooking on low heat for 30 minutes.

Meanwhile make the putu: In a saucepan, bring water to a boil. When water begins to boil, add 1 teaspoon of salt and polenta, stirring constantly. Continue cooking and stirring polenta until mixture begins to thicken, about 3 to 5 minutes. Reduce heat to medium and continue cooking, stirring occassionally, until polenta is smooth and creamy. Spoon polenta onto large platter. Pour vegetable mixture in the middle of the polenta. Serve hot.

Can also be served in individual bowls.

I recently had a party with an "Out of Africa" theme. I wanted to make some food to go with the theme, so I called a friend of mine, Myrna White, who had been a missionary in Africa for twenty years. I used the ideas that she gave me to develop this recipe. It is delicious! —Cinda

*An African word for polenta.

Serves 8 to 10

Per serving: Cal. 111   Fat 3.4g   Sat. fat 0.5g   Sod. 586mg   Carb. 18.7g   Diet. Fiber 3.3g   Prot. 3g

Vegetable Pot Pie

Roll out a little more than half of the pie crust and fit into an 8-inch square baking dish.

In a large skillet over medium heat, sauté onion in olive oil until translucent. Add mushrooms. While this is cooking, add the seasonings. When mushrooms are tender, approximately 3 to 5 minutes, add the frozen mixed vegetables and continue cooking.

Tear the FriChik into small chunks and add to the vegetables along with all the FriChik gravy.

Mix soy milk, flour, and salt together until well blended. Add to the vegetable mixture and continue cooking. Stir constantly until thickened, a minute or two at most. Remove from heat. Stir in Better Than Sour Cream. Pour into the pastry-lined baking dish.

Roll out remaining crust and top baking dish. Cover edges with foil. Bake at 400 degrees for 1 hour. Let cool 10 minutes before serving.

I have always been fond of pot pie, but this one is my favorite! It is easy to make, and the flavors blend together very nicely. I like to serve it with mashed potatoes, green leafy salad, and homemade wheat dinner rolls.
—Cinda

1 recipe of your favorite pie crust

Olive oil

1 small onion, diced

2 cups finely chopped fresh mushrooms

1 teaspoon Vege-Sal

1½ teaspoons McKay's Chicken Style Seasoning

1 teaspoon McKay's Beef Style Seasoning

1 32-ounce package frozen mixed vegetables

1 12.5-ounce can Worthington FriChik, undrained (or your favorite gluten)

3 cups original flavor Better Than Milk soy milk

¾ cup Wondra flour

1 teaspoon salt

3 tablespoons Tofutti Better Than Sour Cream

Yields 10 to 12 servings

Per serving: Cal. 316 Fat 16.5g Sat. fat 1.6g Sod. 584mg Carb. 34g Diet. Fiber 5.1g Prot. 9.5g

Vegetable Cacciatore

2 medium onions,
   sliced thin

1 tablespoon olive oil

2 medium sweet red
   peppers,
   sliced thin

3 cups sliced
   mushrooms

1 medium zucchini,
   sliced

1 medium yellow
   squash

1 1-quart can diced
   tomatoes

1 package Good
   Seasons Italian
   Dressing Mix

6 cups cooked rice or
   pasta

In a large skillet over medium heat, sauté onions in oil until translucent. Add peppers, mushrooms, zucchini, and yellow squash to the onions and continue cooking until almost tender. Add tomatoes and dressing mix. Simmer for approximately 15 minutes. Serve hot over rice or pasta.

Add any of your favorite vegetables—broccoli, Brussels sprouts, okra, green beans, lima beans . . . —Brenda

Serves 8 to 10

Per serving: Cal. 202 Fat 2.7g Sat. fat 0.4g Sod. 485mg Carb. 40.6g Diet. Fiber 4.9g Prot. 5.1g

Cayman Islands Barbecue FriChik

In a large skillet over medium heat, heat olive oil and sauté onion, peppers, and celery until tender. Add Scotch Bonnet Pepper Sauce, liquid aminos, and Pickapeppa Hot Sauce.

Cut FriChik pieces into 4 to 6 pieces each. Add to vegetable sauté, covering FriChik. Marinate approximately one hour. Stir in pineapple. Place in a medium-size baking dish and cover with barbecue sauce or sweet and sour sauce. Bake for 15 to 20 minutes at 350 degrees.

One of my family's favorite vacations is to visit our friends, Gene and Melissa Thompson, in the Cayman Islands. There is nothing quite like good family bonding time while scuba diving in God's underwater Eden. Of course, swimming in "sting ray city" with Gene is an adventure in itself! Every evening we relax and converse while enjoying a wonderful meal. Melissa also likes to cook and has shared some of her recipes with me. This Cayman Islands Barbecue FriChik is a delicious blend of her ideas and mine. —**Cinda**

1 to 2 tablespoons olive oil

1 large sweet onion, diced

1 red pepper, diced

1 yellow pepper, diced

3 stalks celery, diced

Dash Scotch Bonnet Pepper Sauce

2 to 4 tablespoons Bragg Liquid Aminos

2 to 4 tablespoons Pickapeppa Hot Sauce

2 12.5-ounce cans Worthington FriChik or your favorite gluten

1 small can pineapple chunks, drained

1 to 1½ 18-ounce jars barbecue sauce or sweet and sour sauce

7 cups cooked rice

Yields 14 ½-cup servings

Per serving: Cal. 227   Fat 4.9g   Sat. fat 0.7g   Sod. 651mg   Carb. 37g   Diet. Fiber 2.8g   Prot. 8g

Potato-Vegetable Pie

6 to 8 medium
   potatoes, peeled
   and sliced

2 cups sliced carrots

Pastry crust of your
   choice (double
   pie crust, phyllo
   dough, or puff
   pastry sheets)

1 large onion, diced

2 16-ounce packages
   water-packed
   firm tofu, rinsed
   and crumbled

2 8-ounce containers
   herb and chive
   flavor Tofutti
   Better Than
   Cream Cheese

2 packages Good
   Seasons Italian
   Dressing Mix

1 10-ounce package
   fresh mushrooms,
   sliced

1 large package fresh
   spinach

1 cup soy milk

Place potatoes in a large kettle, cover with water, and bring to a boil. Lower heat to a slight boil and cook until potatoes are tender. Drain.

In a medium saucepan over medium heat, cook carrots in 1 cup of water until tender, watching to make sure carrots do not cook dry.

Line springform pan with half the pastry crust of your choice, set aside. (Remaining crust will go on top of pie.)

In a large skillet over medium heat, sauté onion until translucent. Add crumbled tofu, Better Than Cream Cheese, and Italian dressing mix. Remove from skillet.

Place mushrooms in skillet and sauté till tender, add spinach. Continue cooking until spinach is completely wilted and soft. Add tofu mixture and soy milk to spinach mixture. When heated, set aside.

In a pastry-lined springform pan, layer 1/3 potatoes, 1/3 spinach mixture, and then 1/3 carrot slices. Repeat layers till pan is full.

Prepare remaining crust for top of pie. Cut vents into top crust. (*I always cut out a little design—usually a flower—on the top crust before placing on pie.*) Place crust on top of pie. Seal and flute edges. Protect fluted edges with foil. Bake in oven at 350 degrees for approximately 1 hour, until crust is golden.

When baked, remove from springform pan and place carefully on a round platter. Garnish with fresh parsley around the bottom of pie and place cherry or grape tomatoes every two inches around pie.

Slice in wedges and serve hot! —**Brenda**

Yields 8 to 10 1/2-cup servings

Per serving: Cal. 531   Fat 33g   Sat. fat 5g   Sod. 872mg   Carb. 46g   Diet. Fiber 4g   Prot. 15g

Desserts

Fruit Pizza Dessert
p. 100

Pecan
Crescents
p. 102

Lemon Chiffon Pie
p. 94

Applesauce
Carrot Cake
p. 98

Blueberry Pie

5 cups frozen
    blueberries

1 6-ounce can frozen
    apple juice
    concentrate

½ cup unbleached
    white flour

¾ teaspoon cinnamon

1 pie crust
    (recipe below)

PIE CRUST:

⅔ cup canola oil

5 tablespoons ice
    water

2 cups flour

½ teaspoon salt

In a large bowl, combine blueberries, apple juice concentrate, flour, and cinnamon. Mix together and set aside.

Make pie crust (directions below). Gently divide pie crust dough in half. (Too much handling of dough makes it tough.) Roll out between two pieces of wax paper into a round circle a couple inches bigger than the pie pan. Place in pie pan and add filling. Roll out the other half of dough. Use leaf cookie cutters and cut shapes out of the dough. Place on top of the filling. Completely cover the top of the pie with leaf dough shapes. (You can use any shape cookie cutter you like or just cover with another rolled out round top crust. If using a rolled out top crust, pinch bottom and top crusts together, turn under slightly and then "flute" the edges all around the pie.) If you are feeling really creative, cut out shapes freehand!

Bake at 350 degrees for approximately 1 hour, until top of crust is golden.

For pie crust: In a medium mixing bowl, combine oil and ice water. Whip together until it appears cloudy.

In a measuring cup, mix together flour and salt. Slowly stir flour mixture into oil mixture. Use the crust as directed in the recipe.

I got this pie crust recipe from my mother-in-law, Aggie Johnson. I shared her recipe with a friend who has always had a hard time making pie crust. She tried this recipe and was excited because it was the first time she had ever been able to make a good pie crust. This recipe helps make pie crust-making fun, even for the kids. —Linda

Yields 8 slices

Per slice: Cal. 394 Fat 19.8g Sat. fat 1.5g Sod. 145mg Carb. 50.9g Diet. Fiber 3.9g Prot. 4.5g

Frozen Carob-Peanut Butter Pie

In blender, blend tofu, 3/4 cup of peanut butter, honey, oil, vanilla, and salt until smooth and creamy. Set aside.

In a glass bowl, spread 1 cup peanut butter evenly, covering bottom and sides of bowl. Add carob chips. Microwave approximately 1 minute, until melted. (Do not overheat because the mixture will harden, curdle, and become unusable.) Stir together until smooth. Add cereal. Spread carob mixture into baked pie shell. Freeze approximately 4 hours, until set.

Pour peanut butter/honey mixture into pie shell and return to freezer until completely frozen.

Serve just slightly thawed. Garnish with carob curls and/or chopped peanuts.

This pie is also good served with a graham cracker crust. If you omit the carob, you have a plain peanut butter pie! I like to make two at a time—one for now and one for later. Will keep frozen for two to three months.
—Brenda

- 1 baked pie shell
- 1 12-ounce package firm Mori-Nu Tofu
- 3/4 cup plus 1 cup peanut butter
- 1/2 cup honey
- 1/4 cup oil
- 1 teaspoon vanilla
- 1/4 teaspoon salt
- 2 cups barley-sweetened carob chips
- 1 1/2 cups crisp rice cereal

Yields 12 slices

Per slice: Cal. 491 Fat 34g Sat. fat 10.4g Sod. 418mg Carb. 39.4g Diet. Fiber 4.9g Prot. 15.3g

Lemon Chiffon Pie

1 cup Florida Crystals Milled Cane Sugar

⅓ cup cornstarch

1 4-ounce package Mori-Nu Mates Lemon Creme Pudding Mix

⅛ teaspoon salt

2 cups cool water

1 cup fresh squeezed lemon juice (approximately four large lemons)

2 teaspoons soy margarine

Grated rind of two lemons

1 9-inch baked pastry pie shell or prepared graham cracker shell

Nondairy whipped topping

Lemon slices or raspberries for garnish

In a saucepan, mix the dry ingredients together. Whisk in the water and lemon juice and bring to a boil over medium heat. Cook 3 to 5 minutes, stirring often with a whisk. Remove from heat. Stir in the margarine and grated lemon rind. Let the filling cool for about 20 minutes. Pour into pie crust and chill 4 to 6 hours, or until firm.

Serve with nondairy whipped topping and thin lemon slices.

I like to serve this light dessert to my family and friends for a special Sabbath treat. It is especially delightful when garnished with a sprinkle of fresh raspberries on top of the nondairy whipped topping. —Linda

Yields 8 slices

Per serving: Cal. 307 Fat 9.7g Sat. fat 3g Sod. 170mg Carb. 53.5g Diet. Fiber 0.5g Prot. 1.6g

Pumpkin Swirl Cheesecake

Prepare graham cracker crust: In a medium mixing bowl, combine all ingredients. Mix together and press into the bottom and sides of an 8- or 9-inch springform pan. Set aside.

In a large mixing bowl, mix together Better Than Cream Cheese and ½ cup Florida Crystals. Remove 1 cup of the cream cheese mixture to a separate small bowl. Set aside.

In the large bowl, add tofu and whip together until smooth and creamy. Add remaining ingredients (including the remaining Florida Crystals) and mix on high speed for 4 to 5 minutes. Pour mixture into crust. On top of the pumpkin, swirl in the 1 cup of cream cheese mixture. (If the cream cheese mixture is too hard to swirl, microwave for a few seconds until soft enough to swirl on top.) Filling should look marbled.

Bake at 350 degrees for 1½ hours, or until a toothpick inserted in the middle of the cheesecake comes out clean. Center should appear nearly set when shaken. Take out of the oven and cool completely on a wire rack. Chill at least 4 hours before serving.

Just before serving, dip a knife into hot water and slide it around the sides of the pan. Lift off the springform ring. Cut into wedges. Garnish each serving with a dollop of nondairy whipped topping and a few fresh raspberries.

This recipe is excellent for those events when you are wanting something extra special. —**Linda**

Serves 12 to 16

GRAHAM CRACKER CRUST:

- 1 cup graham cracker crumbs
- 4 tablespoons pecan meal
- 1 tablespoon whole-wheat pastry flour
- 1 tablespoon Florida Crystals Milled Cane Sugar
- ½ cup soy margarine

Graham cracker crust (recipe at left)

- 2 8-ounce containers Tofutti Better Than Cream Cheese
- ½ cup plus ½ cup Florida Crystals Milled Cane Sugar
- 1 12.3-ounce package soft Mori-Nu Silken Tofu
- 1 15-ounce can pure pumpkin
- ½ teaspoon cinnamon
- 3 tablespoons Clear Gel*
- 1 teaspoon vanilla
- ¼ cup Dressler's Soy Good Soy Beverage Powder (or any sweet soy milk powder)
- Nondairy whipped topping and fresh raspberries for garnish

*A precooked, dried form of cornstarch to thicken cold liquids.

Per serving: Cal. 231   Fat 15g   Sat. fat 4.4g   Sod. 307mg   Carb. 21g   Diet. Fiber 0.6g   Prot. 4.5g

Pharaoh's Carrot Cake

½ cup canola oil

1½ cups Sucanat Granulated Cane Juice or Florida Crystals

1 8-ounce can crushed pineapple, undrained

3 cups finely grated carrots

¼ cup shredded coconut

½ cup water

2 teaspoons natural vanilla

1 cup raisins

2 cups whole-wheat pastry flour

1 cup unbleached flour

1½ tablespoons Rumford's Baking Powder

1½ tablepoons Ener-G baking soda

1 teaspoon salt

1 teaspoon coriander

¼ teaspoon cardamom

½ teaspoon cinnamon

½ cup chopped walnuts

1 cup Florida Crystals Milled Cane Sugar

Fluffy Frosting (recipe at right)

FLUFFY FROSTING:

1 8-ounce container Tofutti Better Than Cream Cheese

4 cups nondairy whipped topping

In a large bowl, combine oil, Sucanat, and undrained crushed pineapple. Mix together until the Sucanat is completely dissolved. Add carrots, coconut, water, vanilla, and raisins. Mix until well blended.

In a separate bowl, combine flours, baking powder, baking soda, salt, spices, and walnuts. Gradually add wet ingredients to dry ingredients, mixing well until blended.

Spray a 15 x 10-inch jellyroll pan with nonstick cooking spray; line with parchment paper or wax paper. Spray the paper also. Spread batter on top of paper and bake at 350 degrees for 30 minutes.

Put 1 cup of Florida Crystals Milled Cane Sugar into a blender and blend until it is a powder. Sprinkle most of the powdered Florida Crystals onto a clean tea towel, and then invert hot cake onto towel. Peel off paper and gently roll up cake and towel together, starting with narrow end. Cool on a wire rack.

When cooled, gently unroll and spread with Fluffy Frosting (directions below). Roll cake again. Wrap in plastic and refrigerate at least 1 hour before slicing. Sprinkle with the remaining powdered sugar before serving.

For Fluffy Frosting: In a medium mixing bowl, beat cream cheese with a hand mixer until fluffy. Mix in nondairy topping.

One year for my husband's birthday, I gave him a party with an Egyptian theme to honor "the ancient one!" I created this version of his favorite, carrot cake, and named it in honor of him, my pharaoh for the evening. Can freeze for later if desired. —Cinda

Serves 12 to 15

Per serving: Cal. 374 Fat 16g Sat. fat 3g Sod. 848mg Carb. 56g Diet. Fiber 4g Prot. 4g

Tofu-Carob Mousse Cake

In blender, combine tofu, maple syrup, soy milk powder, and water. Blend until smooth.

Melt carob chips in double boiler. Pour melted chips into other ingredients in blender. Blend until smooth.

Cover bottom of a 9 x 13-inch pan with graham crackers. Spread 1/3 of the carob mousse over the top. Add another layer of graham crackers and top with another 1/3 of the mousse. Finish with a layer of graham crackers and remaining mousse.

Grate carob on top of pie. Chill in refrigerator overnight.

Cut into squares and garnish with raspberries. —**Linda**

2 12.3-ounce packages soft or silken Mori-Nu Tofu

2 tablespoons pure maple syrup

1/4 cup soy milk powder

1/4 cup water

1 1/2 cups carob chips plus extra for garnish

25 to 30 graham crackers (approximately 1 1/2 boxes)

Fresh raspberries for garnish

Yields 12 to 15 pieces

Per piece: Cal. 197 Fat 6.6g Sat. fat 5g Sod. 236mg Carb. 29.7g Diet. Fiber 2.5g Prot. 7.3g

Applesauce Carrot Cake

2 cups whole-wheat
    pastry flour

2 cups unbleached
    white flour

1 tablespoon
    Rumford's
    Baking Powder

1 teaspoon salt

3 teaspoons cinnamon

½ cup soy milk powder

1 cup Sucanat
    Granulated
    Cane Juice

1 cup pure maple syrup

1 cup canola oil

1 cup water

1 teaspoon vanilla

2 tablespoons
    applesauce

4 cups grated carrots

1½ cups chopped nuts

Frosting (recipe below)

Walnut halves and
    pieces for garnish

Grated carrots for
    garnish

FROSTING:

1 cup pure maple syrup

1 8-ounce container
    Tofutti Better
    Than Cream
    Cheese

In a mixing bowl combine flours, baking powder, salt, cinnamon, soy powder, and sugar. Mix together. Make a well in the middle of the dry ingredients and add maple syrup, oil, water, vanilla, and applesauce. Mix together and blend until creamy. Fold in carrots and nuts.

Spray two 9-inch round pans with nonstick cooking spray and divide cake batter evenly between the two pans.

Bake at 350 degrees for 32 minutes. Cake is done when toothpick inserted into the middle of the cake comes out clean. (Be careful not to overbake. This is a very moist cake.)

Take the cake out of the oven and place on a cooling rack for 10 minutes. Go around the edge of the cake with a knife. Place a plate on top of the cake and flip the cake over onto the plate. Take another plate and do the same to the other cake. Cool completely.

For the frosting: In a saucepan over medium heat, cook maple syrup until it changes to a creamy color. Remove from heat and stir in Better Than Cream Cheese. Mix until well blended.

Put a small amount of frosting on one of the cakes. Flip the other cake on top of that one. Pour the rest of the frosting on top and let a little dribble down the sides.

Garnish with walnut halves all the way around the edge of the cake. Put a walnut half in the middle and a couple of teaspoons of grated carrot around the walnut. Sprinkle chopped walnuts on the cake. —**Linda**

Serves 12 to 15

Per serving: Cal. 546 Fat 28g Sat. fat 3g Sod. 355mg Carb. 71.3g Diet. Fiber 3.7g Prot. 6.4g

Homespun Ivory Cake

In a medium mixing bowl or measuring cup, combine flour, baking soda, and salt; set aside.

In a separate bowl, mix egg replacer and 1/4 cup water; set aside.

In another bowl, mix soy milk and 1/2 cup water; set aside.

In a large mixing bowl, beat margarine with electric mixer until creamy. Gradually add sugar until well creamed. Beat in vanilla. Add mixed dry ingredients alternately with the soy milk mixture and egg replacer mixture, beating after each addition. (Begin and end with the dry ingredients.) Pour batter into two 8-inch round cake pans that have been sprayed with a nonstick cooking spray and lightly floured. Bake at 375 degrees for 30 to 35 minutes, or until wooden pick or knife inserted comes out clean.

2¾ cups all-purpose white flour

2½ teaspoons Ener-G baking soda

½ teaspoon salt

2 teaspoons Ener-G egg replacer

¾ cup soy milk

½ cup soft soy margarine

1¾ cups Florida Crystals Milled Cane Sugar

1½ teaspoons natural vanilla

This is your basic white cake, without the dairy! Ice with your favorite frosting. Serve with fresh fruit or as the base for strawberry shortcake.
—**Cinda**

Yields 12 to 16 slices

Per serving: Cal. 188   Fat 5.9g   Sat. fat 1g   Sod. 394mg   Carb. 32g   Diet. Fiber 0.5g   Prot. 1.8g

Fruit Pizza Dessert

4 cups oatmeal cookie dough (recipe of your choice)

2 8-ounce containers Better Than Cream Cheese

2 tablespoons honey or maple syrup

3 cups fresh fruit

Suggestions: raspberries, strawberries, blueberries, kiwi, mandarin orange sections, pineapple

On a round baking sheet, spread oatmeal cookie dough into a circle approximately 12 inches in diameter. Bake as directed until golden. The cookie should be soft after baking—not crisp! Transfer to a round platter while cookie is still warm, using spatulas. Cool completely. Set aside.

In a mixing bowl, combine cream cheese and honey or syrup. Spread this mixture onto cooled cookie. Arrange fresh fruit on top to decorate. (Avoid fruits that turn dark quickly.)

Cut into wedges and serve on a dessert plate. Pizza may be prepared 1 to 2 hours before serving.

You can have lots of fun with this recipe. Sometimes I make individual-sized cookies and decorate each differently. You can also use nuts, raisins, apricots, or other dried fruits. Your imagination is your only limit! —**Brenda**

Yields 12 slices

Per serving: Cal. 329   Fat 19g   Sat. fat 5g   Sod. 312mg   Carb. 36g   Diet. Fiber 2g   Prot. 4g

Roxana Jam Cookies

Mix all ingredients (except jam) together. Drop by tablespoon onto cookie sheet.

Bake at 350 for 8 to 10 minutes, until lightly browned. While cookies are still warm, press a spoon in the center of each cookie to make an indention. When cooled, fill indention with a small spoonful of your favorite jam.

When my sisters and I recorded our CD, the wife of our graphics designer baked us some cookies. They were warm right from the oven and delicious. This is not her exact recipe but is so close that I named these cookies, "Roxana Jam Cookies" in her honor! —**Cinda**

1 cup Florida Crystals Milled Cane Sugar

½ cup margarine

½ cup Better Than Milk powder, vanilla flavored

1 teaspoon Rumford's Baking Powder

½ cup water

2 cups flour

Jam of your choice

Yields 36 cookies

Per cookie: Cal. 79 Fat 1.6g Sat. fat 0.2g Sod. 43.6mg Carb. 15.3g Diet. Fiber 0.2g Prot. 1.0g

Pecan Crescents

¾ cup whole-wheat pastry flour (more as needed for shaping crescents)

¼ cup cornstarch

⅛ teaspoon salt

½ teaspoon baking powder

½ cup toasted chopped pecans

¼ cup maple syrup

3 tablespoons canola oil

1 teaspoon vanilla

1 recipe carob dip (recipe below)

1 cup chopped pecans

CAROB DIP:

1 cup barley-sweetened carob chips

1 cup creamy natural peanut butter

Sift flour, cornstarch, salt, and baking powder. Add toasted pecans.

In a separate mixing bowl, whisk oil, maple syrup, and vanilla with a fork. When blended, pour into dry ingredients, stirring with a fork until the mixture holds together. (Dough should be moist and sticky.) Set the dough in a small covered container or seal in plastic bag. Chill in the freezer for 30 minutes until completely cold, or refrigerate for 4 hours.

When dough is chilled, place oven rack in middle of oven. Preheat oven to 400 degrees. Line a cookie sheet with parchment paper.

Remove half the dough, leaving the rest in the freezer or refrigerator. Roll 1 tablespoon dough between the palms of your hands into a log about 3 inches long. Curve into a crescent shape as you place it onto the parchment paper. (If the dough feels sticky, lightly flour your hands.) Repeat with remaining dough. Bake 9 to 13 minutes, until slightly golden and the tops feel fairly firm but yield slightly to gentle pressure. Remove cookie sheet from oven and allow crescents to cool completely.

When cool, remove from parchment paper. Dip just one end of each crescent into carob dip (directions below) and then into chopped pecans, and return to the parchment paper. Place in freezer for 3 to 4 minutes, until carob is firm to the touch. Store in an airtight container at room temperature for up to five days.

For carob dip: Spread peanut butter in glass bowl, covering bottom and sides of bowl. Place carob chips in middle of bowl. Melt on high in microwave for 1 minute. Let set for 1 minute and then stir melted chips and peanut butter together until smooth.

These cookies have a crispy, crumbly texture! They are not a moist, chewy cookie. I like to make a double batch and keep some in the freezer for my grandson, Michael, who loves them. That way I have them on hand whenever he is at "Grandma's house." You can also freeze these cookies for up to three months. —**Brenda**

Yields 12 to 14 crescents

Per serving: Cal. 295 Fat 22.5g Sat. fat 4.2g Sod. 151mg Carb. 21g Diet. Fiber 4g Prot. 7.6g

Carob-Peanut Butter Balls

In a medium bowl, combine peanut butter, granola, salt, and vanilla. Dip hands into water to prevent dough from sticking to your hands. Form dough into 1-inch balls. Roll in coconut and/or finely chopped nuts. Set aside.

In a double boiler, melt carob chips. Dip balls into the melted carob. Place on cookie sheet lined with waxed paper. Freeze for 3 to 4 minutes, until carob is hard to the touch. They are ready to eat at this point, or can be frozen until later.

I sometimes add raisins for variety. You can also pour mixture into a square pan, cover with carob, and cut into squares if you wish! —Brenda

Makes 19 1-inch balls

½ cup natural peanut butter

2 cups granola

Pinch of salt

1½ teaspoons vanilla

Coconut or finely chopped nuts

2 cups barley-sweetened carob chips

Per ball: Cal. 155   Fat 9.7g   Sat. fat 3.6g   Sod. 162mg   Carb. 15g   Diet. Fiber 3.4g   Prot. 5.4g

Peanut Butter Fudge

In a medium mixing bowl, mix peanut butter and honey until smooth and creamy. Add remaining ingredients, mixing well. Spread in a 9 x 9-inch pan. Refrigerate until completely cold.

Cut into 1-inch squares and store in an airtight container. This fudge can be stored in refrigerator for 4 to 6 weeks. It also freezes well.

I love recipes that have very few ingredients. Even the most insecure cook is not intimidated by this recipe! —Brenda

Yields 81 1-inch squares

1 cup peanut butter

⅓ cup honey

1 cup soy milk powder

½ teaspoon pure vanilla

½ cup chopped walnuts (optional)

Per serving: Cal. 35   Fat 2g   Sat. fat 0.3g   Sod. 21mg   Carb. 3.6g   Diet. Fiber 0.2g   Prot. 1.4g

Yummy Popcorn

½ cup unpopped
   popcorn
½ cup dry roasted
   peanuts
¼ cup molasses
¼ cup natural peanut
   butter
¼ teaspoon salt

Pop popcorn in an air popper.

In a large mixing bowl, combine popcorn and peanuts and set aside.

In saucepan over medium heat, stir together molasses, peanut butter, and salt. Heat until just blended together. Drizzle over popcorn and peanuts, mixing until well coated. Put on baking sheets and bake 1½ hours at 200 degrees, until crispy! —**Linda**

Serves 4

Per serving: Cal. 346   Fat 18.4g   Sat. fat 3g   Sod. 296mg   Carb. 40g   Diet. Fiber 2.5g   Prot. 11g

Frozen Fruit Shakes

3 cups frozen peaches
1 cup frozen
   raspberries
1 cup frozen
   blueberries
1 cup frozen
   strawberries
1 to 2 cups white
   grape juice
   or soy milk

Place fruit in blender, using any combination of fruit that you like. Add enough grape juice and/or soy milk until desired consistency is reached. Shake should be smooth and liquid enough to drink through a straw.

These shakes can be made ahead of time and frozen. Just leave time for them to thaw slightly before serving. If you add less liquid, you can serve mixture slightly frozen in a dish as a sorbet. The great thing about this recipe is that you can add or take away just about any fruit that you want to. I like a "peach shake" with just peaches. Experiment to make your own favorite shake! —**Brenda**

Yields 8 8-ounce servings

Per serving: Cal. 87   Fat 0.3g   Sat. fat 0.2g   Sod. 2.3mg   Carb. 22g   Diet. Fiber 3.3g   Prot. 1g

Family Favorites

Eggless
Dinner Rolls
p. 113

Swedish
Rusks
p. 127

No-Bake Tofu "Cheesecake"
p. 123

**Vegetable
Prinavera
p. 114**

Introduction to Family Favorites

Every family has their own traditional recipes that make each gathering extra special, and our family is no exception. We have lots of fun in the kitchen cooking together, each preparing a favorite recipe to be shared by all. In this section of *Cooking With the Micheff Sisters,* we want to introduce you to some of the members of our family.

Dad (1) enjoys cooking, and we love his creations, especially his casseroles and pasta dishes. Mom (2) has always been our inspiration in the kitchen. Everything that she makes is seasoned with love. We think that you will find her recipes appetizing and affordable.

Our brother Ken (3) is a great cook. His food is delicious, and there is never a dull moment in the kitchen when he is cooking. He cooks with style, flair, and a whole lot of fun.

Ken's wife Tammy (3) is also a wonderful cook. When we visit at her home, she always has a pot of soup and homemade bread waiting for us.

Our sister-in-law Gail (4) is the vegan queen in our family. Our brother Jim (4) can tell you that she can make anything taste great!

Catie (5), Cinda's daughter, has taken her mom's love for cooking to heart. She enjoys spending time in the kitchen creating her own nutritious recipes. She hosts her own cooking segment on 3ABN's "Kids Time."

And let's not forget Linda's mother-in law, Aggie (6), who is famous for her melt-in-your-mouth dinner rolls.

We hope that you enjoy our family favorites as much as we do!

In a medium saucepan over medium heat, bring soy milk to a boil. Remove from heat and stir in sugar, salt, and margarine. Cool to lukewarm (105 to 115 degrees).

Warm a large mixing bowl by running under warm water; dry completely. Add warm water to the bowl. Sprinkle in dry yeast; stir until dissolved. Add lukewarm milk mixture and 3 cups flour. Beat by hand or with mixer until smooth. Beat in additional flour to make dough stiff.

Turn dough out onto a floured board and knead about 2 minutes, until dough can be formed into a ball. Place kneaded dough in a clean mixing bowl sprayed with a nonstick cooking spray. Cover and let rise 1 hour. Punch dough down and divide it in half.

On a board heavily sprinkled with cornmeal, put each half of dough. Pat or roll out to ½-inch thickness. Cut into circles with a floured 3-inch cookie cutter. Place on ungreased baking sheets about 2 inches apart. Cover and let rise about ½ hour, until double.

Place on a lightly greased medium hot griddle or a skillet that has been sprayed with a nonstick cooking spray, cornmeal side down. Bake until well browned, about 10 minutes on each side. Cool on wire racks. To serve, split muffins in half and toast.

1 cup soy milk

2 tablespoons Florida Crystals Milled Cane Sugar

1 teaspoon salt

3 tablespoons soy margarine

1 cup warm water (105 to 115 degrees)

1 tablespoon dry yeast

5 to 6 cups unbleached flour

Cornmeal

These muffins can be kept frozen for approximately four to six weeks. I like to have them handy for breakfast, although they are good with any meal. They make wonderful "pizza spins." Just slice them in half and spread with spaghetti sauce and any vegetables that you like. Top with soy cheese and place under broiler till soy cheese is golden in color. Serve hot! —**Bernice**

Yields 18 muffins

Per serving: Cal. 152   Fat 2.5g   Sat. fat 0.4g   Sod. 150mg   Carb. 28g   Diet. Fiber 1.2g   Prot. 4.2g

Home-ground Wheat Bread

6 cups warm water

½ cup honey

½ cup olive oil

1 tablespoon lecithin granules

¼ teaspoon vitamin C powder

½ cup cooked oatmeal

½ cup applesauce

1 tablespoon salt

11 cups Montana red wheat berries, ground into flour, or 7 cups fresh whole-wheat flour

3 to 4 tablespoons instant dry yeast

In stand mixer* bowl, combine water, honey, oil, lecithin, vitamin C powder, oatmeal, applesauce, and salt. Add flour and turn on mixer to lowest speed setting. Add yeast. Add additional flour until dough cleans the side of the bowl. At that point, set a timer for 10 minutes. Continue mixing. Add a small amount of flour during this time as needed to prevent the dough from sticking to the sides of the mixing bowl.

When the 10 minutes are up, form dough into seven loaves. Place into bread pans sprayed with nonstick cooking spray. Put loaves in cold oven. Let rise for 30 minutes.

Bake at 350 for 30 minutes, until brown. Cool on wire racks.

*If you do not have a stand mixer, use half whole-wheat and half white flour and knead by hand. *(Don't add too much flour during kneading because the bread will turn out dry and tough. I always go a little moist rather than dry.)*

Bread dough may be used for pizza crust, sweet rolls, burger buns, bread sticks, and whatever else your imagination comes up with, so be creative.
—Tammy

Yields 7 average-size loaves

Per loaf: Cal. 800   Fat 21.1g   Sat. fat 2.9g   Sod. 377mg   Carb. 132g   Diet. Fiber 27.2g   Prot. 39g

Lavosh
(ARMENIAN THIN BREAD)

In a large mixing bowl, combine warm water, sesame seeds, wheat germ or bran, melted margarine, salt, honey, pecan meal, and 2 cups flour. Mix until blended. Add instant dry yeast. (It is not necessary to mix yeast with water, just sprinkle it directly into the bowl.) Stir and then allow to rest for 5 minutes.

Mix in flour a little at a time until dough is easy to handle. Turn dough onto a lightly floured surface. Knead dough for approximately 10 minutes, until it is smooth and elastic.

Divide dough into eight parts. Roll each part into a rectangle on a lightly floured breadboard. Lift and turn over as you roll. Use only enough flour to keep the dough from sticking. (The dough should never look floured.) Roll until very thin and then lift onto a cookie sheet. Mark into squares with a pastry cutter or knife. (The thinner the dough is rolled, the better the thin bread will taste.)

Bake at 350 degrees for 10 to 15 minutes, until golden brown. The thin bread squares closest to the edge of the pan will brown faster, so you will need to remove those squares first.

Try the recipe with all wheat flour or a combination of other flours for variety. These "crackers" freeze well.

Years ago a neighbor made these and brought them to us. Everyone loves them, and they keep so well in the car for those munchies and for the times while waiting for a meal. Be prepared—they disappear fast. —**Bernice**

2 cups warm water

1 cup sesame seeds

1 cup wheat germ
or bran

¼ cup soy margarine,
melted

2 teaspoons salt

1 tablespoon honey

½ cup pecan meal

4 cups unbleached flour
(approximate)

1 package or
1 tablespoon
instant dry yeast

Yields 140 to 160 crackers

Per serving: Cal. 24 Fat 0.8g Sat. fat 0.1g Sod. 32mg Carb. 3.3g Diet. Fiber 0.3g Prot. 1g

Granola

8 cups quick or rolled oats

1 cup coconut

1 cup wheat germ

1 teaspoon salt

1 cup pecans or nuts of your choice

¾ cup water*

¾ cup olive oil*

1 cup Sucanat Granulated Cane Juice

3 tablespoons vanilla

*To reduce fat use 1¼ cup water and ½ cup oil

In a large mixing bowl, combine oats, coconut, wheat germ, salt, and nuts.

In another bowl, combine water, olive oil, sugar, and vanilla. Add to dry mixture. Work mixture with hands, making small clumps. Put mixture onto two cookie sheets.

Bake at 170 degrees overnight or at 250 degrees for several hours. (Turn clumps every half hour if baking at higher temperature.) Granola is done when it is crispy and crunchy.

This delicious cereal is a wonderful "breakfast on the run." Just put some in a baggie. Make fruit parfaits by layering fruit smoothie, fresh fruit, and granola into parfait glasses. —Tammy

Yields 10 to 12 cups

Per serving: Cal. 512 Fat 27g Sat. fat 5g Sod. 186mg Carb. 62g Diet. Fiber 7.6g Prot. 10g

Eggless Dinner Rolls

In a large mixing bowl, combine yeast, honey, and soy milk. Stir until yeast dissolves. Add salt. Gradually add most of the flour, mixing thoroughly. Work in a little more flour by hand as needed until dough no longer sticks to the bowl and is easy to handle.

When dough is well mixed, turn out onto a lightly floured board and knead gently until smooth and elastic. Form the dough into a round ball and place in a large bowl that has been sprayed with a nonstick cooking spray. Cover with a damp cloth. Place in a warm place and let rise until double. Punch down, cover again with the damp cloth, and let dough rise until double. Punch down again.

Spray two 13 x 19 x 2-inch baking pans with a nonstick cooking spray, using enough so that rolls will not stick to the pan. Shape dough into 24 large or 48 small rolls. Place rolls in pans and cover with the damp cloth and let rise.

When doubled in size, bake 15 to 20 minutes at 350 degrees.

I use this basic recipe to make sweet rolls, hamburger buns, or pizza crust. These inexpensive dinner rolls are light, fluffy, and delicious and will add extra eating pleasure to any meal. —**Aggie Johnson, Linda's mother-in-law**

2 tablespoons active dry yeast

½ cup honey

1¾ cups warm soy milk (80 to 85 degrees)

2 teaspoons salt

1 cup whole-wheat flour

4½ cups unbleached white flour (approximate)

Yields 2 dozen large rolls or 4 dozen small rolls

Per large roll: Cal. 160 Fat 1.2g Sat. fat 0.2g Sod. 8.7mg Carb. 31.9g Diet. Fiber 3.8g Prot. 7.9g

Vegetable Primavera

1 tablespoon olive oil

1 large sweet onion, thinly sliced

4 garlic cloves, sliced

1 head broccoli, cut into small florets

3 small zucchini, sliced

3 small summer squash, sliced

2 to 3 cups sliced mushrooms

1 quart home-canned or fresh tomatoes

1 13-ounce can diced low fat FriChik (optional)

1 packet Good Seasonings Italian Dressing Mix

2 teaspoons McKay's Chicken Style Seasoning

Cayenne to taste

Angel hair pasta or basmati rice, prepared according to package directions (about 1 cup cooked pasta or rice per serving)

In a large skillet over medium heat, sauté onions and garlic in olive oil. Add broccoli, zucchini, squash, and mushrooms. Sauté for several minutes. Add tomatoes and FriChik. Season to taste with dressing mix, McKay's Chicken Style Seasoning, and cayenne.

Serve over angel hair pasta or basmati brown rice.

This dish is especially good during the summer when you can get farm-fresh produce. You can use any vegetables that you like or delete any that you don't like! I never make it the same way twice! —Ken

Yields 8 to 10 servings

Per serving: Cal. 289 Fat 3.2g Sat. fat 0.5g Sod. 502mg Carb. 55.6g Diet. Fiber 5.7g Prot. 11.5g

Capusta

In a large skillet over medium heat, add water to shredded cabbage until just covered. Sauté until tender. Season with salt and soy margarine to taste.

Cook noodles according to package instructions and drain. Add to the cooked cabbage and mix well.

For color, I sometimes add shredded carrots to the cabbage while cooking. This recipe was one that my mom always fixed. She grew up in Hungary, and she learned how to fix it from her grandmother. I loved it as a little boy, and I fixed it for my kids when they were growing up. This recipe has been in the family for many years, and it is so easy to make! —James Micheff

1 medium head cabbage, shredded

Shredded carrots (optional)

Salt to taste

Soy margarine to taste

1 pound fettuccine noodles, broken in thirds, cooked, and drained

Yields 6 to 8 servings

Per serving: Cal. 165 Fat 2.3g Sat. fat 0.4g Sod. 407mg Carb. 31.1g Diet. Fiber 4.5g Prot. 6.2g

Cabbage Rolls

1 medium onion, diced

1 tablespoon olive oil (to taste)

2 cups vegeburger of your choice or homemade gluten *(recipe on p. 80)*

1 tablespoon McKay's Beef Style Seasoning

1 teaspoon salt

3 cups uncooked white rice

1 medium head cabbage (leaves should not be split or cracked)

1 quart canned tomatoes (home-canned if available)

In a large skillet over medium heat, sauté onion in olive oil until translucent. Add vegeburger and seasonings. Stir to mix; add uncooked rice and mix well. Set aside.

In a large kettle over high heat, boil water. Core cabbage and remove outer leaves, reserving them. Remove kettle from heat. Place cabbage in boiling water to cover. With tongs, remove leaves as they wilt—they should be tender, not cooked. Drain.

Shave the vein of the leaf with a sharp knife so that it will not be so thick, being careful not to cut all the way through. Hold the cabbage leaf in your hand with the vein end facing you. Place a tablespoon of rice mixture in the middle of the leaf and fold half the leaf over the top of the rice. Then roll up and tuck the other end inside to make a firm roll.

Line the bottom of a heavy Dutch oven with outer cabbage leaves to prevent scorching. Layer cabbage rolls in pan and top with half the tomatoes. Add another layer of cabbage rolls and pour the rest of the tomatoes on top. Add water around the edges until level with, not covering, the tomatoes. Cook over medium-low heat approximately 1 hour. (Cooking on the stove top is better than trying to bake in the oven.) Check often to avoid boil over. Add more water as necessary.

Variations: If you like sauerkraut, sprinkle a little over each layer.

Rice mixture can also be put into hollowed out red, yellow, orange, or green peppers and cooked with tomatoes using the same kind of pan as the cabbage roll. (Red peppers are the best!)

Another way to use the rice mixture is to make Spanish rice by cooking in taco sauce and tomatoes using a large covered skillet. Simmer over low heat until rice is tender.

Cabbage rolls are the most requested dish whenever there is a family gathering or special event. Even birthdays are not complete without a pot of cabbage rolls. The dish isn't hard to make, so try it, and it might become your family's favorite too! —**Bernie**

Yields 15 to 20 rolls

Per roll: Cal. 313   Fat 3.7g   Sat. fat 0.3g   Sod. 645mg   Carb. 57g   Diet. Fiber 6.4g   Prot. 13g

Dad's Noodle Casserole

In a large kettle, cook and drain noodles according to package directions. Set aside.

Drain FriChik and reserve broth. Shred FriChik. In a large skillet over medium heat, sauté mushrooms in margarine. Stir in flour and gradually add soy milk and FriChik broth, stirring to prevent lumps. Remove from heat. Stir in seasonings and Sour Supreme. Mix all ingredients together and put in a 9 x 13-inch casserole dish. Top with bread or cracker crumbs or a sprinkle of dried parsley flakes.

Bake at 350 degrees 30 to 45 minutes, until lightly browned.

This is another recipe that I love to make and is a favorite of my grandkids. Sometimes I add 1 to 2 cups of frozen peas or broccoli. Try adding your favorite vegetable for something different! —James

1 pound fettuccine noodles, broken in thirds

1 12.5-ounce can Worthington Low-fat FriChik

2 cups fresh mushrooms

¼ cup soy margarine

⅓ cup flour

2 cups soy milk

Garlic salt to taste

1 teaspoon McKay's Chicken Style Seasoning

1 8-ounce container Tofutti Sour Supreme

Bread or cracker crumbs or dried parsley (optional)

Yields 8 servings

Per serving: Cal. 372 Fat 12g Sat. fat 3g Sod. 378mg Carb. 49g Diet. Fiber 2.8g Prot. 14.6

Macaroni & "Cheese"

1½ cups plus ½ cup seasoned bread crumbs

1 cup raw cashews

2½ cups water

1 2-ounce jar pimentos

2 tablespoons fresh lemon juice

1 teaspoon onion powder

2 teaspoons salt

1 teaspoon garlic powder

3 cups macaroni

In a blender, combine all ingredients (except the macaroni and approximately ½ cup of seasoned bread crumbs) and blend until very smooth.

Cook and drain macaroni according to package directions. Place in a greased 9 x 13-inch pan. Pour the cashew/pimento mixture over the top, making sure that all of the macaroni is coated.

Bake, covered, at 350 degrees for 30 minutes. Uncover and sprinkle the seasoned bread crumbs on top. Bake uncovered for 15 more minutes.
—Gail

Yields 10 to 12 servings

Per serving: Cal. 242 Fat 9.3g Sat. fat 1.9g Sod. 728mg Carb. 35.5g Diet. Fiber 1.9g Prot. 7.4g

Brown Rice Casserole

1 cup uncooked brown rice

2 cups diced carrots

2 stalks celery, diced

1 medium onion, chopped

1 teaspoon dried parsley

1 teaspoon salt

1 tablespoon McKay's Chicken Style Seasoning

1 can diced FriChik, undrained

4 cups water

Mix all ingredients together and put in a greased 9 x 13-inch pan with a cover. Bake covered at 350 degrees for 1 to 1½ hours until rice is fluffy and liquid absorbed.

As a pastor's wife, I go to many church potlucks, so I'm always looking for recipes that taste great but don't require a lot of time. This recipe is so easy to make and I always come home with an empty dish! —Gail

Yields 8 servings

Per serving: Cal. 170 Fat 1.1g Sat. fat 0.2g Sod. 3630mg Carb. 33.8g Diet. Fiber 1.9g Prot. 3.8g

In a large mixing bowl, combine flours.

In a large measuring cup, combine seasonings, liquid aminos, and 1 cup tomato juice. Pour over flour and stir until all the flour is moistened. (Gluten develops quickly, so stir quickly.) Place bowl in the refrigerator to chill for 2 hours.

After chilling, use a hand grinder or the grater blade of a food processor to grind walnuts, then onion, and then gluten. (Grind more than once if needed.) Mix well and then knead a minute or so by hand.

In a casserole dish that has a lid, shape the roast mixture as you would a meatloaf, leaving space all around. Pour 2 cups tomato juice on the top and bake at 350 degrees for 1 hour.

Remove lid and bake another 15 minutes, until a little brown on top. Remove from oven, place on top of the stove, and re-cover. Let sit for 30 minutes while steam finishes the cooking.

When I take this roast to a potluck I always have one or two requests for the recipe. Leftovers make excellent cold sandwiches. —**Bernie**

- 2 cups vital gluten flour
- ½ cup whole-wheat pastry flour
- 2 teaspoons McKay's Beef Style Seasoning
- ½ teaspoon garlic powder
- 2 tablespoons yeast flakes
- 3 tablespoons Bragg Liquid Aminos
- 1 cup plus 2 cups tomato juice
- 1 cup walnuts
- 1 large onion, quartered

Yields 8 to 10 servings

Per serving: Cal. 216 Fat 8g Sat. fat 0.7g Sod. 221mg Carb. 16.4g Diet. Fiber 2g Prot. 22g

Yum for the Tum Potatoes

8 large potatoes

½ cup Wondra or all-purpose flour

3 cups Better Than Milk soy milk or soy milk of your choice

1 8-ounce container Tofutti Better Than Cream Cheese, herb and chive flavor

Soy margarine to taste

Salt to taste

Peel potatoes and place in large kettle. Cover with water and bring to a boil. Boil gently until tender. Allow to cool completely.

Meanwhile, in a shaker container, shake flour and soy milk until well mixed. Pour into a saucepan and cook over medium heat until slightly thickened. Stir in Better Than Cream Cheese and margarine until well mixed.

Slice cooled potatoes and add to sauce. Stir gently until mixed well. Pour into baking dish and bake at 350 degrees for approximately 30 minutes, until bubbly.

My Mom began to teach my brother David and me how to cook when we were very young. She had us helping her stir and mix everything she prepared. We loved standing beside her helping her create new recipes and make our old favorites. She always made it fun for us and never seemed to mind the messes we made. She even made clean-up fun! My mom instilled in both my brother and me her love for cooking. During the holidays you will find all four of us (yes, my dad cooks too!) in the kitchen each creating our own recipes. This dish is one of my favorites. —Catie

Yields 12 servings

Per serving: Cal. 166 Fat 6.6g Sat. fat 1.5g Sod. 103mg Carb. 23g Diet. Fiber 2.4g Prot. 4.8g

In a large saucepan, mix together apple concentrate and cornstarch. Over medium heat, cook until thickened and clear, stirring frequently. Stir in apples and cinnamon. Set aside.

In a large mixing bowl, combine flours and salt.

In a measuring cup, combine oil and water. Add oil and water to flour, stirring gently into a soft ball. (Overworking the dough makes the crust tough.) Divide dough in half. Between waxed paper or plastic wrap, roll dough into a circle to fit a 9-inch pie plate.

Line 9-inch pie plate with dough, trimming dough that hangs over the edge of the plate. Pour in filling. Roll out remaining dough. Cut a design or slits for steam vents. Place on top of pie. Crimp bottom and top crusts together.

Bake at 350 for 30 to 45 minutes, until crust is golden.

You may substitute any fruit for the filling. The apple juice concentrate brings out more of the "apple" taste and is just the right amount of sweetener. It is also good to use with other fruits because the taste doesn't overwhelm them. —**Tammy**

1 12-ounce can apple juice concentrate

2 tablespoons cornstarch

6 cups thinly sliced apples

1 teaspoon cinnamon

1 cup white flour

1 cup whole-wheat pastry flour

1 teaspoon salt

½ cup olive oil

5 tablespoons ice water

Yields 8 slices

Per slice: Cal. 320   Fat 15g   Sat. fat 2g   Sod. 280mg   Carb. 46g   Diet. Fiber 5.3g   Prot. 3.5g

Pumpkin Pie

1 12-ounce package
firm Mori-Nu
Tofu

1 cup water

1 can pumpkin

¾ cup Sucanat
Granulated
Cane Juice,
or ⅔ cup honey
or other
sweetener

½ teaspoon salt

1½ teaspoons
cinnamon

¾ teaspoon ginger

¼ teaspoon nutmeg

¼ teaspoon cloves

Unbaked pie shell

In a medium mixing bowl, blend tofu and water together until smooth. Add remaining ingredients (except for pie shell) to tofu mixture. Mix well and pour into unbaked pie shell.

Bake at 350 degrees for 1 to 1½ hours, until knife inserted in center comes out clean. Best served cold. —Gail

Yields 8 slices

Per slice: Cal. 226 Fat 8.6g Sat. fat 4.5g Sod. 284mg Carb. 33.4g Diet. Fiber 2g Prot. 5g

No-Bake Tofu "Cheesecake"

In a springform pan, press graham cracker crust mixture, prepared according to recipe instructions. Set aside.

In a saucepan over medium heat, combine juice concentrate with Emes Jel. Stir until gelatin is dissolved. Pour into blender, add cashews, and blend until satiny smooth. Add rest of ingredients and blend smooth. Pour gelatin mixture into the prepared crust. Chill at least 2 hours.

Remove "cheesecake" from pan and place on a cake plate or serving platter. Serve with your favorite toppings.

I like to serve this "cheesecake" with fresh fruit. Berries are especially good.
—Gail

Graham cracker crust
  (Recipe on p. 95)

1¼ cups Dole frozen pineapple-orange juice concentrate

3 tablespoons Emes Kosher-Jel

½ cup raw cashews

⅓ cup honey

2 12-ounce packages firm Mori-Nu Tofu

½ teaspoon salt

½ teaspoon lemon juice

1 cup coconut milk

Yields 8 to 10 servings

Per serving: Cal. 284 Fat 16.6g Sat. fat 8.6g Sod. 365mg Carb. 27g Diet. Fiber 0.7g Prot. 8.7g

Apple Burritos

8 apples, coarsely
chopped

⅓ cup water

¼ cup raisins

1 teaspoon pure
vanilla

⅛ teaspoon maple
flavoring

6 tortillas

1¾ cups plus ¼ cup
apple juice

2 cups pineapple juice

¼ cup arrowroot or
cornstarch

Toasted coconut
(optional)

In a large saucepan, add apples, water, raisins, vanilla, and maple flavoring. Cook over medium heat until apples are softened.

Fill tortillas with apple mixture and roll up. In a 9 x 13-inch casserole dish, place filled burritos seam side down.

In a medium saucepan, combine 1¾ cups apple juice and pineapple juice. Bring to a boil.

In a measuring cup combine ¼ cup apple juice and arrowroot or cornstarch. Add to heated juice in saucepan. Reduce heat to simmer and stir constantly until thickened.

Pour sauce over burritos and bake at 350 degrees for 30 minutes. Sprinkle toasted coconut over top just before serving, if desired.

Variations: Add ½ cup chopped walnuts to filling. For peach burritos, substitute 1 quart diced fresh peaches for the apples and use 4 cups peach juice for the liquid. —**Bernice**

Yields 6 burritos

Per burrito: Cal. 458   Fat 5.8g   Sat. fat 1.4g   Sod. 341mg   Carb. 98g   Diet. Fiber 7g   Prot. 7g

Carob Fudge

Spread peanut butter on the bottom and up the sides of a microwave-safe bowl. Add carob chips and microwave for 1 minute only. Stir until all the carob chips are melted. Spread in a greased 8-inch square pan and refrigerate until firm. Cut into 1-inch squares.

Variations: Add 2 cups of any of the following in any combination: Crisp rice cereal, coconut, nuts, raisins, or mashed granola pieces. —**Gail**

Yields 64 pieces

1 cup natural peanut butter

2 cups barley-sweetened carob chips

Per serving: Cal. 39 Fat 2.9g Sat. fat 1.0g Sod. 13mg Carb. 2.8g Diet. Fiber 0.7g Prot. 1.5g

Carob Joy

In a medium mixing bowl, mix together honey, oat bran, coconut, carob powder, salt, vanilla, water, and ½ cup peanut butter. Mix well with hands. Shape into 1 x 2-inch bars—like candy bars. Press two or three toasted almonds on the top.

Spread 2 tablespoons peanut butter on bottom and sides of a microwave-safe bowl. Place carob chips in bowl on top of the peanut butter. Microwave for 1 minute. Let rest a minute and then stir. (The peanut butter helps the chips to melt smoothly.) Spoon the melted carob over the candy bars. This will hold the almonds in place. Freeze.

Carob Joys are ready to eat right from the freezer.

You'll want to make a double batch so that you can keep extra in the freezer. Papa loves to have me keep these in the freezer for whenever he thinks he needs something sweet, which is quite often. —**Bernice**

Yields 48 bars

1 cup honey

3 cups oat bran

2 cups unsweetened coconut

¼ cup carob powder

Scant ½ teaspoon salt

2 tablespoons pure vanilla

4 tablespoons water (approximate)

½ cup soy milk powder

½ cup plus 2 tablespoons peanut butter

Toasted almonds

1 cup barley-sweetened carob chips

Per bar: Cal. 101 Fat 4.7g Sat. fat 1.8g Sod. 63mg Carb. 16g Diet. Fiber 1.8g Prot. 3.8g

Carob-Date Fudge

1 cup chopped dates

¼ cup carob powder

1 cup peanut butter

1 cup chopped
walnuts

1 teaspoon vanilla

½ cup shredded
coconut

In a medium saucepan over high heat, bring ½ cup water to a boil. Turn down heat and add dates, stirring until thick and almost smooth.

In another saucepan over high heat, bring another ½ cup water to boil. Lower heat, add carob powder, and stir for 5 minutes, till a smooth paste forms. Mix the softened dates and the rest of the ingredients into the carob paste. Pour the mixture into an 8-inch square pan. Cover and refrigerate. Cut into 1-inch squares when cool. —**Gail**

Yields 64 pieces

Per serving: Cal. 45 Fat 3.5g Sat. fat 0.7g Sod. 3.5mg Carb. 3.1g Diet. Fiber 0.5g Prot. 1.3g

Swedish Rusks

In a large bowl, combine soy milk, salt, sugar, margarine, and yeast. Add enough flour to make dough you can handle. Place on flat surface.

Knead dough until smooth and elastic, approximately 10 minutes. Add enough flour while kneading to keep hands from getting sticky. Let dough rise until double in size. Punch down and shape into baguettes. Let rise until double in size.

Bake at 350 degrees for approximately 30 minutes, until tops of loaves are golden. Cool completely.

Slice loaves into ½-inch thick slices. Place bread slices on cookie sheet. Bake slowly at 250 degrees until completely dry and crispy. (Do not overbake. Rusks should be barely golden in color when done.) Store in an airtight container for 4 to 6 weeks.

4 cups soy milk, warmed to 70 or 80 degrees

1 teaspoon salt

2 cups Florida Crystals Milled Cane Sugar

2 sticks margarine

3 tablespoons instant dry active yeast

5 pounds bread flour (approximate)

A Swedish church member used to bake these for our children when they were little, and they just loved them. I have revised the recipe to omit dairy products, and the bread still turns out delicious! These rusks are meant to be hard and crispy and are great snacks. They are also good for teething babies!
—Bernice

Yields 12 dozen rusks

Per rusk: Cal. 88   Fat 1.8g   Sat. fat 0.3g   Sod. 32.5mg   Carb. 15.3g   Diet. Fiber 1.1g   Prot. 3.2g

Cooking
for a
Crowd
With Linda

Apple Pie
p. 147

Lasagna
p. 148

Fettuccine With
Alfredo Sauce
p. 149

Black Olive
Salad
p. 150

Breakfast Menu for 50

Whole-Wheat Pecan Pancakes

SLICED STRAWBERRIES*

HOT BLUEBERRY SAUCE

NONDAIRY WHIPPED TOPPING*

SOY MARGARINE*

PEANUT BUTTER*

Scrambled Tofu

Granola

Orange Juice*

Soy Milk*

Ingredient quantities and instructions for menu items without recipes:

Sliced strawberries:
2 5-pound containers (comes frozen)

Nondairy whipped topping:
1 32-ounce can Rich's Topping (this comes frozen and will need to be whipped)

Soy margarine:
2 pounds

Peanut butter:
5 pounds

Orange juice:
3 gallons for one 7-ounce serving per person

Soy milk:
3 gallons for one 7-ounce serving per person (most of the time 2 gallons are enough)

Whole Wheat-Pecan Pancakes

Mix all the dry ingredients and pecans together in a large bowl. Make a well in the middle and pour in the remaining ingredients. Gently stir everything together until batter is well mixed. If the batter is on the thick side, gradually add more water, up to two cups. (Be cautious—if the batter is too thin, the pancakes will come out more like crepes.)

Fry over medium heat on a grill sprayed with a nonstick cooking spray or in a nonstick skillet. Pancakes are ready to flip when they are bubbly on top. Pancakes should be a light golden brown. Stack the pancakes to keep them hot.

Serve with blueberry sauce (directions below) and nondairy whipped topping.

Variations: Instead of blueberry sauce, use a strawberry sauce (directions below) or hot applesauce and peanut butter.

For blueberry sauce: Bring juice and blueberries to a boil. In a separate bowl, stir cornstarch into cold water until well blended. While stirring the boiling juice, slowly add the cornstarch mixture. Stir until thickened. Remove from heat and stir in the cinnamon. Cover until ready to serve.

Strawberry sauce variation: Make strawberry sauce by substituting strawberries for the blueberries, omitting the cinnamon, and using apple juice in place of grape juice. Prepare fresh strawberries (frozen work too) and set aside. Bring apple juice to a boil. Stir in the cornstarch mixture as in the blueberry sauce recipe. When thickened, remove from heat and add strawberries. Top with nondairy whipped topping.

8 ⅓ cups unbleached white flour

8 ⅓ cups whole-wheat flour

½ cup Soy Good Soy Milk Powder (or any sweet soy milk powder)

2 teaspoons salt

½ cup Rumford's Baking Powder

4 cups chopped pecans

14 cups plus 2 cups water

2¾ cups canola oil

2 cups maple syrup

2 cups unsweetened applesauce

BLUEBERRY SAUCE:

24 cups apple or grape juice

16 cups blueberries

1 cup cornstarch

2 cups cold water

2 teaspoons cinnamon

Per serving: Cal. 445 Fat 19g Sat. fat 1.5g Sod. 320mg Carb. 66g Diet. Fiber 5g Prot. 6g

Scrambled Tofu

12 pounds water-
   packed firm tofu

2 cups hot water

5 cups sliced green
   onions

12 12.3-ounce
   packages firm
   Mori-Nu Tofu

3 cups nutritional
   yeast flakes

½ cup McKay's
   Chicken Style
   Seasoning

½ cup McKay's Beef
   Style Seasoning

¼ cup Vege-Sal,
   optional

1 tablespoon garlic
   powder

Fresh parsley

Tomato slices

Imitation bacon bits

Drain and rinse tofu in cold water. In a jellyroll pan, set the tofu to drain further. Cover with plastic wrap and place something heavy on top to squeeze out as much liquid as possible. Let sit for about 10 to 20 minutes.

In a large skillet, put hot water and green onions. Let them simmer until all the water is gone, watching carefully to keep from burning.

Meanwhile, in a large bowl, crumble all the tofu. Add seasonings and stir. Add seasoned tofu to the onion mixture. Cook over low heat for 25 to 30 minutes, stirring every 5 minutes.

Garnish with fresh parsley, tomato slices, and imitation bacon bits.

Leftover scrambled tofu can be used in fried rice or burritos. It is a good alternative to scrambled eggs and, unlike eggs, is low in cholesterol.

Per serving: Cal. 151   Fat 6.5g   Sat. fat 5.6g   Sod. 596mg   Carb. 8g   Diet. Fiber 1.5g   Prot. 16g

Granola

In a large bowl, combine oats, salt, coconut, and nuts.

In a blender, combine water, oil, vanilla, and Sucanat. Blend mixture well. Pour mixture over dry ingredients. Mix until all ingredients are moist. (If the mixture feels too wet, add a little more oatmeal. If it feels too dry, add a little more water, but not too much because it will change the texture of the granola.) Squeeze some of the mixture together, making clumps the size of pecans. Pour granola mixture onto cooking sheets and bake at 250 degrees for 2 to 3 hours, turning occasionally until granola is slightly browned and crisp. Cool and store in an airtight container. Store in refrigerator to keep longer than a week.

This granola is simple and easy to make. I serve it with any combination of blueberries, strawberries, peaches, raspberries, raisins, and dates. It makes a hearty breakfast.

4 gallons quick oats

4 teaspoons salt

4 cups coconut

4 cups nuts

5 cups water

4 cups canola oil

¾ cup vanilla

4 cups Sucanat Granulated Cane Juice

Per serving: Cal. 624 Fat 28g Sat. fat 4g Sod. 196mg Carb. 83g Diet. Fiber 10g Prot. 13g

Picnic Supper Menu for 50

Barbecue Vege-Beef
HOMEMADE BUNS*
SLICED ONIONS*
SLICED PICKLES*

Potato Salad

Roasted Corn

Watermelon*

Pecan Soynut Butter Cookies

Grape Juice*

*Ingredient quantities
and instructions for
menu items without
recipes:*

Homemade buns:
50

Sliced onions:
10–15 large onions

Sliced pickles:
1 gallon

Watermelon:
3 large (20 servings
per watermelon)

Grape juice:
6 gallons (14 ounces
per serving)

Barbecue Vege-Beef

In a microwave-safe bowl, combine onions and ¾ cup water. Microwave for 6 to 8 minutes, until onions are translucent.

Mix all ingredients together.

Spray two 13 x 22-inch baking dishes with nonstick cooking spray. Divide barbecue mixture between the two pans. Cover and bake at 350 degrees for one hour.

Serve with homemade buns, sliced onions, and pickles.

* I use Westbrae Natural Fruit Sweetened Catsup, available in the health food section of a large grocery store or in a health food store.

3 medium onions, finely diced

¾ cup water

15 cups tomato sauce

5 cups fruit-sweetened catsup*

⅔ cup Bragg Liquid Aminos

3½ tablespoons Vege-Sal or seasoned salt, optional

3½ tablespoons Sucanat Granulated Cane Juice

12 1-pound, 4-ounce cans Worthington Vegetarian Burger

5 cups imitation bacon bits, optional

Per serving: Cal. 191 Fat 5g Sat. fat .01g Sod. 1430mg Carb. 16g Diet. Fiber 3.6g Prot. 23g

Potato Salad

20 pounds potatoes, cooked and diced

3 cups diced pickles

2 cups sliced green olives

9 cups Vegenaise

3 tablespoons Vege-Sal or seasoned salt

1 tablespoon salt

1½ tablespoons onion powder

Radish roses, parsley, carrots or imitation bacon bits for garnish

Place potatoes in a large bowl. Add pickles and green olives.

In another bowl, combine Vegenaise with Vege-Sal, onion powder, and salt and stir to mix. Stir into the potato mixture. Chill for about 4 hours before serving. After chilling, taste to see if the salad needs more seasoning.

This salad is best if made the day before you want to serve it because the seasonings have time to blend. I sometimes add 1 to 2 cups black olives to this recipe. Celery, carrots, and radishes can also be added. However, I have found that the simpler the foods are prepared, the easier it is to please large groups of people.

Per serving: Cal. 418   Fat 27g   Sat. fat 4.5g   Sod. 913mg   Carb. 41g   Diet. Fiber 3.5g   Prot. 3.3g

Place unhusked corn in a large container and cover with salted cold water. Soak for 8 hours.

Put 6 inches of sand in each half of the barrel. Cover the sand with foil, letting the foil lap up the sides of the barrels. Place charcoal on top of the foil and light. Place the grates on top of the half barrels. Let the charcoal burn for 15 to 20 minutes, and then place the unhusked corn on top of the grates. After approximately 10 minutes turn the corn over and roast for approximately 10 more minutes and serve. Corn may be kept hot in a big, covered pan.

This can also be done on grills if there are enough of them to accommodate 100 ears of corn. If corn is the main item on the menu, roast more than two per person.

100 ears unhusked corn

1 cup salt

TOOLS:

1 steel barrel, cut in half lengthwise

Sand

Foil

Charcoal

Lighter fluid

Matches

Grates

Per serving: Cal. 165 Fat 2g Sat. fat 0.3g Sod. 388mg Carb. 38g Diet. Fiber 4.3g Prot. 5g

Pecan Soynut Butter Cookies

5 cups roasted soynut butter

5 cups canola oil

5 cups pure maple syrup

½ cup vanilla

2½ cups water

15 cups unbleached white flour

5 cups whole-wheat pastry flour

½ cup Rumford's Baking Powder

5 cups chopped pecans

5 cups carob chips

Blend soynut butter, oil, syrup, vanilla, and water together until creamy. Slowly mix in the dry ingredients. Stir in the pecans and carob chips.

Spray cookie sheets with nonstick cooking spray. Using a small scoop (#50), place dough on the cookie sheet. Flatten in a crosshatch pattern with a fork. Bake at 350 degrees for 12 to 15 minutes, until lightly browned. Remove the cookies from the cookie sheet and place them on a cooling rack.

These cookies are quick and easy to make. They freeze well. Make peanut butter cookies by substituting natural peanut butter for the soynut butter and omitting the pecans and carob chips.

Yields 200 cookies.

Per cookie: Cal. 179 Fat 11g Sat. fat 1.4g Sod. 93mg Carb. 18g Diet. Fiber 2.2g Prot. 4g

Dinner Menu for 50

Lentil Nut Balls
    With Brown Gravy

Brenda's Potato Florentine Baskets

French Green Beans Amandine*

Corn*

Homemade Dinner Rolls
    SOY MARGARINE*

Carrot-Raisin Salad

Strawberry Shortcake
    NONDAIRY WHIPPED TOPPING*

Lemon Water*

*Ingredient quantities
and instructions for
menu items without
recipes:

French Green Beans
    Amandine:
    10 pounds frozen
    or canned green
    beans and one
    pound roasted
    silvered almonds
    to be combined
    just before serving

Corn:
    10 pounds frozen
    or canned

Soy margarine:
    2 pounds

Whipped topping:
    1 2-pound can
    Rich's Topping
    (will need to be
    whipped)

Lemons:
    6, thinly sliced

Lentil Nut Balls

14 cups cooked lentils, drained well

10 cups seasoned bread crumbs

2 cups pecan meal

3 cups chopped walnuts

1 tablespoon Vege-Sal, optional

2 tablespoons McKay's Beef Style Seasoning

1 teaspoon onion powder

1 medium onion

2 12.3-ounce packages firm Mori-Nu Tofu

2 8-ounce containers Tofutti Better Than Cream Cheese

½ cup Bragg Liquid Aminos

Olive oil

Brown gravy (recipe below)

BROWN GRAVY:

1 gallon cool water

3 to 4 tablespoons McKay's Beef Style Seasoning

Salt to taste

1 cup Bragg Liquid Aminos or soy sauce

1 medium onion

3 cups white flour

1 cup canola oil

In a mixing bowl combine lentils, bread crumbs, pecan meal, walnuts, Vege-Sal, beef-style seasoning, and onion powder. Stir together.

In a blender, combine onion, tofu, Better Than Cream Cheese, and liquid aminos. Blend until smooth and add to the lentil mixture. Stir together. Let rest in the refrigerator approximately 20 minutes.

Spray cookie sheets with nonstick cooking spray. Put a little olive oil on your hands and roll lentil mixture into 1-inch balls; place on cookie sheet. (Lentil mixture should be fairly firm. If not, add a few more seasoned bread crumbs.) Bake at 350 degrees for 45 to 60 minutes, turning halfway through baking time. Balls are done when browned on both sides and firm to the touch. Put the balls in a baking dish and cover with brown gravy (directions below). Bake for 30 to 40 minutes, until hot and bubbly.

Lentil balls can be made ahead and frozen for future use. This recipe can also be made into a loaf by adding 2 cups Grape Nuts and _ cup canola or olive oil. Bake at 350 degrees for about 1 hour.

For brown gravy: In a kettle, mix together water, beef-style seasoning, salt, and liquid aminos.

In a blender, blend onion and some of the seasoned water. Pour blended onion back into the kettle.

In a skillet over medium heat, brown flour until golden. Allow the browned flour to cool, then sift.

In a separate bowl, mix the flour with oil and 4 cups or more of the seasoned water to make a thin paste. Whip paste into seasoned water and heat on medium high, stirring until it comes to a boil and thickens.

This gravy is fast and easy to make. It has been a favorite at summer camp and for both men's and women's retreats. It can be used with potatoes, patties, and roasts and is also great as a base for vegetable stew or potpie.

Yields 225 to 250 balls / 15 cups gravy

Per serving: Cal. 316   Fat 13g   Sat. fat 2.4g   Sod. 1260mg   Carb. 38g   Diet. Fiber 6g   Prot. 13g

Potato Florentine Baskets

Peel and slice potatoes. Boil potatoes in salted water until tender. Drain and mash. Set aside.

In a skillet over medium heat, sauté onion and garlic in olive oil until onions are translucent. Add mushrooms, spinach, and seasonings. (Use either the dressing mix or the Italian seasonings and salt, not both.) Set aside.

Cut phyllo dough into 4-inch squares. Place one square in a muffin pan cup with ends of dough sticking out. Spray with butter-flavored nonstick cooking spray. Add a second phyllo square on top of the first. Alternate the squares so that the corners are spread evenly around the muffin tin.

In a mixing bowl, combine Sour Supreme and Better Than Cream Cheese. Mix until well blended. Set aside.

Fill phyllo squares in muffin cups with a layer of mashed potatoes, a layer of the spinach mixture, and a layer of the Sour Supreme/Cream Cheese mixture. Finish with a thin layer of mashed potatoes. Bake at 375 degrees for 20 to 30 minutes, until hot and golden brown on top.

This is a great recipe to have your children help with. As the years go by, the memories of cooking together will be a special heritage for your kids.

25 large potatoes

2 tablespoons olive oil

4 onions, minced

¼ cup minced garlic

8 pounds sliced mushrooms

4 5-ounce packages fresh spinach

Good Seasons Italian Dressing Mix or 2 tablespoons Italian seasoning and 2 tablespoons salt

8 packages phyllo dough

5 8-ounce containers Tofutti Sour Supreme

5 8-ounce containers Better Than Cream Cheese

Yields 50 2-basket servings

Per serving: Cal. 310   Fat 13g   Sat. fat 4g   Sod. 843mg   Carb. 40g   Diet. Fiber 3.4g   Prot. 7g

Carrot-Raisin Salad

25 carrots, shredded

2 cups raisins

4 red apples, washed and diced

4 green apples, washed and diced

1 cup chopped pecans

1 12.3-ounce package soft Mori-Nu Tofu

¾ cup Grapeseed Oil Vegenaise

1 teaspoon Vege-Sal

1 teaspoon sweetener

1 pineapple ring

Green leaf lettuce

1 cup pecan halves for garnish

1 seedless green grape for garnish

2 red apples for garnish

2 green apples for garnish

In a large bowl, mix together the carrots, raisins, apples, and pecans.

In a blender, combine tofu, Vegenaise, Vege-Sal, and sweetener. Blend until smooth. Pour over salad and chill for two hours or overnight. Mix well.

To serve, line a large bowl with green leaf lettuce. Fill with carrot salad, being careful not to get any on the lettuce leaves that will show. Garnish with pecan halves and apple slices. Alternate a green apple slice, a red apple slice, and a pecan half around the outside of the salad, working toward the center. Finish the garnish with a pineapple ring and green grape in the center.

This is one of those great salads that can be made a couple of days ahead of time. For variety, add one 20-ounce can of crushed pineapple and substitute the pecans with walnuts or roasted almonds. Use whatever sweetener you like best. I use Splenda.

Per serving: Cal. 104   Fat 5g   Sat. fat 1g   Sod. 64mg   Carb. 14g   Diet. Fiber 2g   Prot. 1.5g

Homemade Dinner Rolls

In an extra-heavy-duty mixer bowl put water, salt, oil, sweetener, oats, yeast, and half the flour. Mix and slowly add enough flour to make a soft dough. Mix for 10 minutes. (To test if it has been mixed enough, roll a small piece of dough in your hands. Dough will be soft, but if it does not stick to your hands, it is ready for the next step. If it does stick to your hands, mix another 5 minutes and test again.)

When dough is mixed, spray the counter with a nonstick cooking spray. Place dough on the sprayed counter. Cover with a towel and let rise until double in size. Cut dough into golf ball-size pieces and roll quickly between the palms of your hands.

In a pan sprayed with a nonstick cooking spray, place dough balls. Cover with a towel and let rise until double in size. Bake at 350 degrees for about 30 minutes. Take out of pan and place on a towel or rack.

8 cups warm water

2⅔ tablespoons salt

1¾ cups canola oil

2 cups sweetener

3 cups cooked quick oats

½ cup active dry yeast

16 cups unbleached white flour (approximate)

10 cups finely ground whole-wheat flour (approximate)

When we sisters were little girls, we loved to help Mom make dinner rolls. She would give us each our own dough and pan. We had so much fun in the kitchen laughing, talking, and enjoying the time together. Sometimes in the midst of our fun, someone passing by would stop and knock on our door. People just couldn't resist the smells of Mom's bread and rolls baking in the oven! Mom would send them away with a freshly baked loaf. And they would always leave with smiles on their faces. Now, whenever we go home, Mom continues to share her love with us (and anyone passing by) with the delightful smells of her homemade goodies.

Yields about 100 dinner rolls

Per roll: Cal. 165   Fat 4g   Sat. fat 0.4g   Sod. 178mg   Carb. 28g   Diet. Fiber 2g   Prot. 4g

Strawberry Shortcake

2 6.5-pound containers frozen sliced strawberries

3 pounds strawberries, sliced plus 50 small fresh strawberries, sliced into fans

8 cups unbleached white flour

4 cups whole-wheat pastry flour

½ cup Rumford's Baking Powder

3 teaspoons salt

1 cup Florida Crystals Milled Cane Sugar

3 cups soy margarine

3¾ cups soy milk

1 2-pound can Rich's Nondairy Topping

50 small sprigs mint for garnish

Mix the frozen and sliced fresh strawberries together in a large bowl and refrigerate until needed.

In a large mixing bowl combine flours, baking powder, salt, and Florida Crystals. Mix together. Cut the margarine into the flour mixture with a pastry cutter or fork until mixture resembles course crumbs. Make a well in the center of the flour mixture. Pour the soy milk into the well all at once.

On a lightly floured surface, knead dough gently for 4 or 5 strokes, just enough to bring the dough together. (The less it is handled, the lighter the biscuits will be.) Roll or pat dough to ½-inch thickness. Cut the dough with a 2½-inch biscuit cutter, dipping cutter into flour between cuts so that the dough will not stick to the cutter.

Spray a cookie sheet or pan with a nonstick cooking spray and place the biscuits so that they touch slightly. Bake at 350 degrees for 25 to 30 minutes. Remove from pan and place on wire rack to cool.

To serve, cut each biscuit in half. Put a tablespoon of nondairy whipped topping on the bottom half of the biscuit. Spoon ½-cup sliced strawberries on top of the whipped topping. Place the top half of the biscuit on top of the strawberries. Top with another tablespoon of the whipped topping. Garnish with a mint sprig and strawberry fan.

Variation: Use sliced peaches in place of the strawberries.

Yields about 50 servings

Per serving: Cal. 350 Fat 11g Sat. fat 2g Sod. 502mg Carb. 61g Diet. Fiber 4.6g Prot. 4.2g

Fellowship Dinner Menu for 50

Lasagna

Fettuccini With Alfredo Sauce

Steamed Fresh Broccoli*

Black Olive Salad
LEMON HERB DRESSING

Home-Style Garlic Bread
SOY MARGARINE*

Apple Pie*

White Grape Juice*

*Ingredient quantities and instructions for menu items without recipes:

Steamed fresh broccoli:
20 pounds (two spears per serving)

Soy margarine:
2 pounds

Apple pies:
make 7 pies from recipe on p. 92, substituting sliced apples for blueberries

White grape juice:
6 gallons for one 14-ounce serving per person

Lasagna (PREPARE THE DAY BEFORE SERVING)

2 large onions, thinly sliced

2 cups water

2 tablespoons plus 2 tablespoons olive or canola oil

4 large red peppers, thinly sliced

8 large carrots, shredded

2 medium zucchini, cut into ½-inch slices

4 large eggplants, peeled and cut into ¼-inch slices

Seasoned flour (recipe on p. 83)

4 12.3-ounce packages firm Mori-Nu Tofu, crumbled into small pieces

2 8-ounce containers Tofutti Sour Supreme

2 teaspoons Italian seasoning

2 teaspoons Vege-Sal, optional

1 teaspoon onion powder

6 1-pound, 10.5-ounce cans low-sodium garlic and herb spaghetti sauce

6 1-pound, 10.5-ounce cans low-sodium chunky vegetable spaghetti sauce

4 1-pound boxes lasagna noodles, uncooked

6 cups sliced black olives

Fresh parsley for garnish

In a microwave-safe bowl, combine onion slices and water. Cover and microwave for 6 to 8 minutes, until translucent.

In a nonstick skillet over medium heat, heat 2 tablespoons olive oil. Add red peppers and sauté approximately 5 minutes. Add carrots and zucchini. Sauté approximately 15 minutes.

On a cookie sheet, spread approximately 2 tablespoons oil. Dip the eggplant slices in the seasoned flour and place on cookie sheet. Bake—on one side only—at 350 degrees for approximately 20 minutes.

In a mixing bowl, mix Sour Supreme into crumbled tofu and mix in Italian seasoning, Vege-Sal, and onion powder.

(Directions are for one pan; repeat in the second.) In an institutional-size pan (20⅞ x 12 ¹³⁄₁₆ x 2-inch) layer the ingredients in this order: 1 can garlic and herb spaghetti sauce; 10 uncooked lasagna noodles; light layer of tofu mixture; 1 cup sautéed vegetables; 1 cup sliced olives; cooked onions; eggplant, unbrowned side down (save enough eggplant for a second layer and the top); 1 can chunky vegetable spaghetti sauce; garlic powder. Repeat for second layer.

Top layer: Uncooked noodles and 2 cans garlic and herb spaghetti sauce. Cut remaining eggplant slices in half and place on top of sauce. Sprinkle with olives. Put pans in refrigerator and let sit overnight to soften the noodles. Bake at 350 degrees for 1 hour. Garnish with fresh parsley.

Variations: Add broccoli and yellow squash to this dish. Sometimes I add approximately 4 cups vegeburger and grate vegan mozzarella cheese on top. And in place of the tofu mixture above, I also add 3 pounds water-packed tofu, drained and crumbled, mixed with 2 8-ounce containers Tofutti Better Than Cream Cheese, 1 container Tofutti Sour Supreme, and 1 tablespoon McKay's Chicken Style Seasoning. This dish is great to make on Thursday night and keep in the refrigerator until Sabbath. It makes Friday preparation for Sabbath so easy!

Per serving: Cal. 424 Fat 14g Sat. fat 2g Sod. 1300mg Carb. 65g Diet. Fiber 7.7g Prot. 11g

Fettuccini With Alfredo Sauce

Cook noodles according to package instructions. Drain and set aside.

In a measuring cup, mix cornstarch and cold water. Set aside.

In a large kettle over medium heat, combine all other ingredients. Bring to a boil, stirring constantly. Add cornstarch mixture to kettle, continuing to stir until sauce is thick. Remove from heat and pour over fettuccini noodles. Garnish with fresh parsley and a cherry tomato. Serve immediately.

Variations: For rice dishes or other recipes that call for a white sauce, omit the vegan parmesan cheese. For imitation bacon gravy, omit the vegan parmesan cheese and the Tofutti Sour Supreme, add a dash of onion powder, 1/4 cup more cornstarch, and 4 cups imitation bacon bits.

10 pounds fettuccini noodles

2 1/2 cups cornstarch

2 cups cold water

24 cups Soy Good Soy Milk, plain (or other plain soy milk of your choice)

3 12-ounce containers Tofutti Sour Supreme

2 1/2 4-ounce jars vegan parmesan cheese

4 1/2 tablespoons Vege-Sal

3 tablespoons soy margarine

Yields 50 servings

Per serving: Cal. 456   Fat 8.6g   Sat. fat 1.8g   Sod. 592mg   Carb. 76g   Diet. Fiber 5g   Prot. 17g

Black Olive Salad

5 heads romaine lettuce

2 heads red leaf lettuce

1 10-ounce package fresh spinach

4 pounds fresh grape tomatoes

5½ cups plus ½ cup black olives

4 cups shredded purple cabbage

4 cups shredded carrots

3 cups banana peppers

4 red peppers, sliced

Cinda's Lemon Herb Dressing (recipe at right)

Radish roses

CINDA'S LEMON HERB DRESSING:

1½ cups fresh garlic cloves

¾ cup Grapeseed Oil Vegenaise

3⅓ cups fresh lemon juice

2 tablespoons salt

3½ tablespoons chervil

3½ tablespoons sweet basil

3½ tablespoons thyme

3½ tablespoons oregano

3½ tablespoons savory

2 tablespoons coriander

3½ tablespoons sage

1⅔ cups water

6⅔ cups extra virgin olive oil

Rinse lettuce, spinach, and tomatoes under cold water. Break lettuce and spinach into bite-size pieces in a large bowl. Add 5½ cups of olives and the remaining vegetables. Mix. Sprinkle ½ cup olives on top of the salad and garnish with radish roses. Serve with Cinda's Lemon Herb Dressing (directions below).

Variation: For a meal in a salad, add 1 cup sunflower seeds, 4 cups chick peas, and 4 cups red kidney beans.

For Cinda's Lemon Herb Dressing: In a blender, combine ingredients except the olive oil. Blend well. Blend at slow speed while adding olive oil. Continue blending until well mixed. Chill dressing in the refrigerator for a couple of hours before serving.

This dressing will keep for a few weeks in the refrigerator. It is great on a fresh green salad!

Per serving: Cal. 315 Fat 33g Sat. fat 4g Sod. 335mg Carb. 5g Diet. Fiber 1g Prot. 1g

Home-Style Garlic Bread

In the bowl of an extra-heavy-duty mixer combine water, salt, honey, oil, whole-wheat flour, yeast, and 16 cups white flour. Mix and let rest for 10 minutes. Slowly add the rest of the flour. Knead in the mixer till smooth and elastic. (If dough sticks to the hands, add just a little more flour.) Let rise until dough is double in size. Punch down and let it rise again.

Spray cookie sheets with a nonstick cooking spray. Form dough into 8 to 10 long loaves and place on cookie sheets. Let rise until double in size. Bake at 350 degrees for about 30 minutes. Remove from oven and pan and cool on cooling racks. Brush with a little olive oil.

Before serving, slice bread, spread slices with soy margarine, and sprinkle each with garlic powder. Wrap loaves in foil and warm in the oven for 15 to 20 minutes.

Bread is also good served warm with olive oil for dipping instead of the margarine and garlic.

10 cups warm water (70 to 80 degrees)

3 tablespoons plus 1 teaspoon salt

1 cup honey

1 cup canola oil

5 1/2 cups whole-wheat flour

10 tablespoons Red Star instant dry yeast (or another brand of your choice)

16 cups plus 16 cups unbleached white flour, approximately

1 cup wheat bran

2 pounds soy margarine

2 1/2 ounces garlic powder

Per serving: Cal. 532   Fat 20g   Sat. fat 3g   Sod. 635mg   Carb. 78g   Diet. Fiber 5g   Prot. 11g

Party Supper Menu for 50

Potato Soup

Cinda's Wheat Crackers

Vegetable Pizza

Black Bean & Potato Pizza

Frosty Fruit Salad

Carob Bars

Pure Apple Juice*

*Ingredient quantities
and instructions for
menu items without
recipes:

Pure apple juice:
   6 gallons for 50
   14-ounce servings

Potato Soup

In a gallon-size kettle combine 8 cups water, potatoes, celery, Vege-Sal, and celery salt. Bring to a boil; then reduce heat to medium.

In a blender combine 1 cup water with onion; blend until the onion is liquified. Add to the soup; cook until potatoes and celery are tender, about 40 to 50 minutes, depending on the size of the kettle. (Always allow more cooking time for larger quantities of food.)

In a blender combine tofu, Better Than Cream Cheese, and soy milk. Pour into soup and stir.

In a measuring cup, combine cornstarch and cold water. Stir. Slowly pour cornstarch mixture into the soup. Stir until thick. Taste the soup to see if it needs more seasoning. (I sometimes add more onion powder and salt.)

Garnish this soup with grated vegan cheese and a little fresh parsley. Good served with your favorite corn bread.

10 pounds potatoes, peeled and diced

4 cups diced celery

7 tablespoons Vege-Sal or to taste

7 tablespoons celery salt or to taste

1 large onion

7 12.3-ounce packages soft Mori-Nu Tofu

4 8-ounce containers herb flavor Tofutti Better Than Cream Cheese

7 cups soy milk

1½ cups cornstarch

2 cups cold water

Vegan cheese for garnish

Fresh parsley for garnish

Yields approximately 70 cups

Per cup: Cal. 147   Fat 7g   Sat. fat 3.5g   Sod. 549mg   Carb. 17g   Diet. Fiber 2g   Prot. 5g

Cinda's Wheat Crackers

15 cups unbleached white flour

5 cups whole-wheat pastry flour

30 cups quick oats

10 cups toasted wheat germ

2 cups Sucanat Granulated Cane Juice

1½ tablespoons salt

10 cups water

7½ cups oil

Mix all dry ingredients and set aside.

Mix the liquid ingredients together and add to dry ingredients until liquid is absorbed.

On cookie sheets, pat or roll dough to ⅛-inch thickness. Cut dough into 2-inch squares and bake at 325 degrees for 20 to 25 minutes, until lightly browned. Watch carefully because crackers tend to burn easily.

There is something special about a pot of homemade soup and Cinda's crackers. She always makes extra for those "drop-in" guests.

Yields 240 crackers

Per cracker: Cal. 159 Fat 8g Sat. fat 0.7g Sod. 42mg Carb. 18g Diet. Fiber 2g Prot. 4g

Vegetable Pizza

For pizza crust: In a stand mixer bowl, combine warm water, salt, sweetener, 7/8 cup oil, 2 cups whole-wheat flour, and yeast. Mix together on low; slowly add the white flour. Continue mixing for 10 to 15 minutes. While still mixing, add the remaining oil. Remove dough from of the mixer bowl and place on a counter with a towel over it. When dough has doubled in size, gently divide the dough among 5 pizza pans. Stretch the dough on the pizza pan until it is the size of the pan. Top with vegetables as listed or your favorite pizza sauce and veggies. Bake at 350 degrees for 25 to 30 minutes, until bottom of crust is a golden brown.

Place eggplant slices in a large bowl. Cover with cold water and add salt.

In a separate bowl, make seasoned flour. Dip the eggplant slices into the seasoned flour and place on an oiled cookie sheet.

In a 350-degree oven, bake eggplant slices on one side only for 20 to 30 minutes, until browned on one side. While eggplant is baking, microwave onions and 2 cups water in a microwave-safe bowl for approximately 10 minutes, until tender. Assemble pizza by covering crust with sauce and lightly sprinkling the sauce with garlic powder. Place vegetables on pizza in any order, reserving eggplant until last. Lay one eggplant slice flour side down on top of the vegetables, placing so that each slice will have one piece of eggplant.

I have served these vegan pizzas for large groups of people, and they have even pleased the "cheese lovers!"

Yields 50 slices

PIZZA CRUST:

- 5 cups warm water (70 to 80 degrees)
- 4 teaspoons salt
- 1 cup date sugar or your favorite sweetener
- 1 cup canola oil
- 4 cups whole-wheat flour
- 5 tablespoons active dry yeast
- 10 cups unbleached white flour

- 1 pizza crust recipe (recipe at left)
- 6 large eggplants, sliced
- 1 teaspoon salt
- Oil
- Seasoned flour (recipe on p. 83)
- 4 1-pound, 10.5-ounce cans low sodium spaghetti sauce
- Garlic powder
- 6 cups sliced black olives, optional
- 4 large onions, sliced
- 5 red peppers, sliced
- 3 yellow peppers, sliced
- 2 pounds fresh sliced mushrooms
- 1 pound fresh broccoli flowerets, steamed

Per slice: Cal. 290 Fat 8g Sat. fat 1g Sod. 1320mg Carb. 45g Diet. Fiber 5g Prot. 7g

Black Bean & Potato Pizza

1 pizza crust recipe
(recipe on p. 155)

4 1-pound, 10.5-ounce
cans spaghetti
sauce

Garlic powder

Potato topping
(recipe below)

4 cups black beans,
drained and
rinsed

POTATO TOPPING:

10 pounds potatoes,
cooked and diced

8 cups diced tomatoes

1 tablespoon salt or to
taste

2 tablespoons Vege-Sal
or to taste

2 tablespoons olive oil

2 large onions, diced

2 tablespoons minced
garlic

1 10-ounce package
fresh spinach

Cover each unbaked pizza crust with spaghetti sauce. Sprinkle garlic powder lightly over the sauce. Spoon on potato topping (directions below). Sprinkle black beans on top of the potato topping. Bake at 350 for 30 to 40 minutes, until crust is golden brown on the bottom.

For potato topping: In a large bowl, combine potatoes, tomatoes, salt, and Vege-Sal. In a skillet over medium heat, sauté onions in olive oil. Add minced garlic. Sauté until onions are clear and can be cut easily with a spoon. Add spinach and simmer for a couple of minutes. Add to ingredients in mixing bowl and combine.

Yields 50 slices

Per slice: Cal. 353   Fat 9g   Sat. fat 1g   Sod. 519mg   Carb. 63g   Diet. Fiber 7g   Prot. 9g

Frosty Fruit Salad

Mix all ingredients together, reserving 2 cups each of blueberries, raspberries, pecans, and kiwis and one whole strawberry. Let the fruit salad chill in the refrigerator for approximately 4 to 6 hours. Just before serving, garnish the salad from the edges, first with the reserved raspberries, then the kiwis, the blueberries, and finally the one strawberry. Sprinkle pecans on top of it all!

This refreshing fruit salad will delight your family and friends. It is also good for us! How wonderful it is that God made so many good things for us to eat!

1 6-pound, 10-ounce can unsweetened pineapple chunks, reserve juice

1 6-pound, 9-ounce can unsweetened peaches, drained

5 pounds small whole strawberries

1 5-pound package frozen mangos

5 pounds red seedless grapes

3 cantaloupe melons, peeled and cubed

1 5-pound package frozen honeydew melon

10 kiwis, sliced

5 pounds frozen blueberries

1 quart fresh raspberries

2 pounds pecan halves

Per serving: Cal. 172 Fat 4g Sat. fat 0.4g Sod. 10mg Carb. 36g Diet. Fiber 5g Prot. 2g

Carob Bars

5 cups all-natural
    peanut butter

5 cups barley-
    sweetened carob
    chips

1 cup maple syrup or
    honey

6¼ cups crisp rice
    cereal

6¼ cups crushed
    granola

5 cups graham cracker
    crumbs

1 cup chopped pecans

Spread the peanut butter on the bottom of a microwave-safe bowl and about 1 inch up the sides of bowl. Place carob chips on top of the peanut butter. Microwave for 1 to 2 minutes on high, until peanut butter is hot. Whip peanut butter and carob chips together. Whip in the syrup or honey. Stir in the remaining ingredients. Pat mixture to ½-inch thickness in two 9 x 13-inch pans. Cut into bars and place pan in the refrigerator. These are best made the day before they are served.

This recipe is a favorite with the kids at summer camp. It is also a quick and easy recipe and fun to make! For a sweeter dessert, add 1 cup diced dates to the recipe.

Yields 55 to 60 bars

Per bar: Cal. 294   Fat 18g   Sat. fat 5g   Sod. 216mg   Carb. 29g   Diet. Fiber 4g   Prot. 9g

Resources

COUNTRY LIFE NATURAL FOODS offers a line of natural, whole, and organic foods at reasonable prices. They carry most of the specialty items in this cookbook, such as Mori-Nu Tofu, Mori-Nu Mates, McKay's Chicken and Beef Seasonings, Bragg Liquid Aminos, Vegex, Emes kosher jel, pure maple syrup, whole grains, herbs, spices, and over 1,200 other natural items. To order, call 1-800-456-7694, and they will ship directly to your house by UPS. Ask for their free catalog.

FOLLOW YOUR HEART is located in Canoga Park, California. They offer Grapeseed Oil Vegenaise and the original Vegenaise. In our opinion these vegan "mayonnaise" products are the best on the market. For more information on where to purchase this product, call 1-818-347-9946 or contact them through their Web site, <www.followyourheart.com>.

AMERICAN NATURAL AND SPECIALTY BRANDS has Better Than Milk soy milk, one of our favorites. We use it in many of our recipes. For more information on this product call 1-800-227-2320 or send email to <info@betterthanmilk.com>.

THREE ANGELS BROADCASTING NETWORK (3ABN) offers a number of health programs. You will be able to view vegan cooking programs and receive additional recipes on 3ABN Television or 3ABN Radio online 24 hours a day. 3ABN's Web site is <www.3abn.org>; their phone number is (618) 627-4651; their email is <mail@3abn.org>; their mailing address is P.O. Box 220, West Frankfort, IL 62896.

TOFUTTI manufactures a variety of nondairy items that are soy based and casein free: Sour Supreme, Better Than Cream Cheese, various soy cheeses, and much more. For more information you can send email to them at <Tofuttibrands@aol.com>, call 1-908-272-2400, visit their Web site at <www.tofutti.com>, or write to them at Tofutti Brands, IC, P.O. Box 786, Cranford, NJ 07016.

MORI-NU's Web site is <www.morinu.com>.

DRESSLER PRODUCTS
Visit <www.dresslerfoods.com> for more information on Soy Good Millk and Soy Add-ums or call 888-526-6330 or write to: Dressler Foods Inc., 184 Panorama Lane, Walla Walla, WA 99362.

YVES Veggie Cuisine product information is available at <www.yvesveggie.com>.

Index